"Ever wish you had a roadmap for navigating the crazy new world of job-hunting? Well, here it is. With a refreshingly honest approach, Jen shares the best ways to find work that fits you like a glove and to turn your gifts into financial rewards. And to top it off, she shows you how to create job security for life. What more can you ask for?"

--Marci Shimoff

#1 *NY Times* Bestselling Author *Happy for No Reason, Love For No Reason, Chicken Soup for the Woman's Soul*

www.MarciShimoff.com

"This book goes beyond just helping you discover what you should be doing; it gives you action steps to develop a strategy to obtain and evolve that perfect career specifically for you so that you can make 'the' difference in the world you want to be making."

--Joan Rott

Director, University of California-Davis Extension

"Jen has provided a powerful, practical and smart approach to using your strengths to forge an exceptional career. Her years of experience as a career coach shine through in every principle and strategy she shares. No matter what your desired income level, when you read this book you will see the path to creating financial independence, achieving personal fulfillment and making a real contribution to the world. Buy a copy now – and buy a copy for everyone you care about."

--Sandy Vilas, MCC

CEO, Coach U, Inc.

"Jen Anderson proves herself to be a Master Gardener with *Plant Yourself Where You Will Bloom!* The world of work has changed dramatically since I started in Human Resources. Jen walks you through the steps needed to make a career and, let's face it, life change in this new environment. She shows you how to take control of your career and find your passion. I wish all of my corporate employees had read this book because their career paths would have been so much easier. Without question, I will be strongly recommending it to my clients from now on. With Jen's keen insight and suggestions, you can do it!"

--Marcie Mortensson, MS, SPHR

Human Resources Executive and Executive Coach

www.YourCoachMM.com


"In *Plant Yourself Where You Will Bloom,* Jennifer Anderson brings her unique combination of expertise as an educator and life coach to book form. Her seven-step career model creates a clear and workable pathway for readers to follow. The real-life stories illustrate that Jen's techniques work and produce tangible results. Her encouraging, positive approach to career change is bound to help a new audience reach their professional goals."

--Dawn Davis

Interim Director, Community Education

Portland Community College


"Most of us have felt, at one time or another, as if we weren't in the best spot to flourish. I know I have. Maybe you feel that way right now. If so, Jennifer's book is the place to find answers; the place to find your way to the best spot for you. How do I know? Because Jennifer helped me through just such a journey. Because of our work together, I've planted myself where

I am not only blooming, but gloriously blossoming. Grab a chair and a cup of tea, and curl up with Jennifer's book. You'll be glad you did."

--Kent Blumberg

Academic Leader, Leadership Coach


"Jen's writing is so real, so honest, and so inviting. It's as if she's speaking directly to you not only about your career but about your passions in life. Her approach is smart and the only way to go in a job market that is constantly changing. This book is a must-read for every smart woman who is ready to discover and articulate their unique gifts and learn how they can share these gifts with the rest of the world. As an educator, I would recommend this book to anyone who is ready to discover their true passion and purpose in life."

--Vivian Miranda

Ed.D. Higher Education Professional


"Jennifer Anderson has helped hundreds of clients have their career epiphany, including myself. *Plant Yourself Where You Will Bloom* is an amazing step-by-step guide to discover and make the transition to your perfect work. Jen asks the powerful questions to help you create awareness on what you REALLY want for your life and your career. She helps you by uncovering the gifts and talents which you already have within you and plant you in a perfect place for you to bloom and thrive."

--Sarah Uchytil, ACC

Life and Career Coach

www.SarahUCoach.com

*Plant Yourself Where You Will Bloom* will put you on the path to career success, which is doing the work you were born to do. Read Jen's book, and start living the life you've always wanted!

--Brian Bartes, Success Coach and Best-Selling Author of

*Life Lessons: A Guide To Creating And Living Your Best Life*

www.lifeexcellence.com

# PLANT YOURSELF WHERE YOU WILL BLOOM

*How to turn what makes you unique
into a meaningful and lucrative career*

Dear Lisa —
You are in
the right work.
Jennifer

## JENNIFER G. ANDERSON

**BALBOA.**
PRESS

A DIVISION OF HAY HOUSE

Balboa Press books may be ordered through booksellers or by contacting:

Balboa Press
A Division of Hay House
1663 Liberty Drive
Bloomington, IN 47403
www.balboapress.com
1-(877) 407-4847

Because of the dynamic nature of the Internet, any web addresses or links contained in this book may have changed since publication and may no longer be valid. The views expressed in this work are solely those of the author and do not necessarily reflect the views of the publisher, and the publisher hereby disclaims any responsibility for them.

The author of this book does not dispense medical advice or prescribe the use of any technique as a form of treatment for physical, emotional, or medical problems without the advice of a physician, either directly or indirectly. The intent of the author is only to offer information of a general nature to help you in your quest for emotional and spiritual well-being. In the event you use any of the information in this book for yourself, which is your constitutional right, the author and the publisher assume no responsibility for your actions.

Printed in the United States of America.

ISBN: 978-1-4525-7860-6 (sc)
ISBN: 978-1-4525-7862-0 (hc)
ISBN: 978-1-4525-7861-3 (e)

Library of Congress Control Number: 2013915003

Balboa Press rev. date: 8/19/2013

# *FREE*
# "FULL BLOOM STARTER KIT"

Jennifer Anderson and the Full Bloom Career Academy
Invite You and a Friend
To register for the free Full Bloom Starter Kit
For more information and to register, please visit
**www.Start2Bloom.com**

Here's what you'll receive:
- **Free E-copy of the acclaimed book:**
  *Plant Yourself Where You Will Bloom*
  How to turn what makes you unique into a meaningful and
  lucrative career
- **Free Career Training:**
  "Who Do You Think You Are?" An introductory guide to
  discovering what makes you unique and how to turn it into a
  lucrative and rewarding career
- **Free Career Audio Training:**
  "The 3 Biggest Mistakes Smart Women Make and what You
  Can Do Instead"
- **$100 Scholarship:**
  Applicable to any career training offered by
  Full Bloom Career Academy
- **Free Client Success Story Recordings:**
  Listen as Jennifer's most successful clients personally describe
  their journeys to meaningful and lucrative careers

**www.Start2Bloom.com**

# ABOUT THE AUTHOR

If something is missing in your career…if you feel you're making far less money than you're worth or that you might not be achieving your purpose in this go-round on the planet—then now is your chance to transform that forever. If you want to discover the work that's a perfect fit for you—that will be personally fulfilling *and* financially rewarding—you don't have to go it alone.

Jennifer Anderson is the founder of Full Bloom Career Academy, a full-service career training and coaching program.

A self-proclaimed "High Tech Refugee," Jen has spent the last 15 years teaching thousands of people the concepts of how to create a thriving career. She's coached hundreds of people down the garden path to discovering their perfect work, and taught hundreds of entrepreneurs the secrets of launching successful small businesses.

An "Early Settler" of the professional coaching industry as well as a Professional Certified Coach, Jennifer is a trainer at Coach University and a faculty member of Portland Community College and the University of California at Davis - Extension.

In the rest of her spare time, Jennifer is a mother of two and a ridiculously proud grandmother of one. She is also an avid fan of University of Kansas Basketball. Rock Chalk, Jayhawk!

In memory of my mother

Mary T. Gibbons

Who made so many beautiful things bloom.

and for my father

Harry C. Gibbons

Who made sure this book bloomed.

# CONTENTS

# INTRODUCTION

Dear Reader,

On a scale of 1-10, with 10 being "everything's coming up roses" and 1 being "I am withering on the vine," just how great is your career?

Do you feel like you're making the difference you want to be making in the world?

Do you feel like you're using your greatest talents on a daily basis?

Do you feel like you're making the money you know you can make and deserve?

Do you feel appreciated for your hard work?

Do you feel grateful each and every day that this is how you make a living?

If you're at less than a 10…if the answer isn't yes to all of these questions…

…Then you are in the perfect place to begin creating a thriving career for yourself.

As you read through this book, my request is that you allow this to be a fun experience filled with curiosity, hope, and inspiration.

What I want for you is a clear direction for your career; an understanding of the gift you're meant to give the world through your work; and a smart strategy for giving it.

With a clear destination, you are far more likely to stay curious and courageous throughout the journey. And in case it helps, I want you to know that…

I believe in you.

I believe you have a deep desire to make a difference in the world. You may be frustrated because you don't know what that difference is. And you may be worried you won't have an opportunity to make that difference.

I believe you have a gift to give.

I believe you came here to give that gift—to somehow make the world a better place because you've been here.

I believe you do everything you can to give that gift, but sometimes in the wrong situations. You might not be appreciated for the gift you're trying to give.

I believe you will live a much more fun and rewarding life when you can articulate your gift, and find the right situations in which to give it.

I believe that your "gift" is the way you go about doing whatever it is that you do best. You don't have to be the best in the world at it. Just do your best.

I believe you give your gift by following your heart.

I believe your gift springs from a vision you hold deep inside. You may not know why it's important to you—it just is.

I believe you can and will discover your gift. And when you do, you'll give it joyfully and reap more rewards than you've ever thought possible.

And that's why I had to write this book for you.


My best to you, always,

Jen

# PROLOGUE

## Plant Yourself Where You Will Bloom

# CHAPTER 1

## *What it Means to*

## *"Plant Yourself Where You Will Bloom"*

Your eyes pop open at the jarring sound of the alarm. You roll over in bed wishing you could go back and finish your dream, but it's too late. You've realized it's Monday morning. Again.

You drag yourself out of bed, splash some water on your face, and take a good look in the mirror.

Who is that stressed-out woman looking back at you? Are those new wrinkles around her eyes? Is that another gray hair?

You glance at your calendar and remember that tonight is girls' night out. It's been three months, and last time when everyone played a round of "why I hate my job" you declared (after finishing off your third martini) that you were definitely looking for new work.

You haven't.

As you commute, you listen to your recorded affirmations and repeat them aloud:

"I am a truly valuable person."

"I complete my work effortlessly and easily."

"People appreciate my hard work."

You park your car, remind yourself to smile, and walk through the office doors determined to make it a good day.

Reaching your desk, you see an unexpected pile of reports that have been dumped, dozens of emails waiting to be answered, and a note that says your boss wants to see you, yet again, about last month's debacle.

Your shoulders slump, you feel the knot in your stomach tighten, and you wonder whether you have the strength to pour yourself a cup of coffee.

*****************

My guess is that you're reading this book because something is off with your work-life.

It may be just a tad off, or you may be light years from where you thought you'd be. No matter what—you're unhappy and know you need to make a change, but you aren't sure how to go about doing it or even what direction to take.

At the same time, you're questioning whether it's wise, given today's unstable economy, to contemplate making a career move. All you have to do is check the online news sources (formerly known as reading the paper) and you can gather all the evidence you need that the world of work is a pretty nasty place, especially for…

…People who are new graduates with no work experience…and people who are no longer in their 20s…and people who are returning to the workforce after an absence…and people who are no longer in their 30s…and people who are being laid off…and people who are no longer in their 40s…and people who are being forced to retire before they want to…and people who are no longer in their 50s…

Hang on! Let's catch our breath.

Yes, it's a competitive career market. And no, you may not have the kind of resume that compels employers to roll out the red carpet and woo you into their corporate inner sanctum.

But the bottom-line remains the same: you're unhappy. And you simply can't continue on in the same way.

Why? Because something is warning you that what you've been doing is no longer working (if it ever really was).

The old approach to making a career choice is about:

• Doing whatever it takes to make the most money

• Following trends—the fields that are expected to grow

• Following in someone's footsteps

• Doing what someone else thinks is best for you

• Taking any job that pays the bills

• Picking a job that allows you to use your talent or your education, or fits in with family commitments, but doesn't consider anything else that is important to you

Can you spot what's missing from this list? Any mention of <u>fulfillment</u>, <u>meaning</u>, or <u>contribution</u>.

If you're just not feeling your work anymore, chances are good that it's missing one or more of these three things.

The old approach to career choice is based on the philosophy of "Bloom where you are planted." The premise is that you should adapt yourself to your situation and make the best of it.

Wow. I must admit that I have a hard time with this!

I'm not saying that this philosophy is never applicable in life. Situations do exist in which you have no power to make a change. You simply have to try to make lemonade out of lemons.

But is that really true about your work? Are you powerless to take charge of your career?

The new approach to choosing a career is based on the philosophy, "Plant yourself where you will bloom." The premise is that you define the work that will fit you like a glove (by discovering and combining your talents, interests, knowledge, values, and preferences regarding people, money, work environment, and lifestyle) and then you use a very specific approach to finding or creating your perfect job.

It's the same as if you want a plant to bloom profusely. Do you drop it on a rock, walk away, and expect to come back in an hour and see a flower? Of course not!

You learn about what it takes for the plant to bloom—things like the best soil conditions and the right amounts of sunlight, water, and fertilizer. You seek out the spot in your yard that easily provides these things. You plant it lovingly. You tend to its needs. And before you know it, it's blooming.

Your ideal work is no different. Your perfect job is the set of circumstances in which the best of you can shine. You love your work, you do the work in a way that fits your integrity, and you live the life you want most.

Maybe at this point you want to jump through the pages, grab me, shake me, and emphatically remind me that you have bills to pay!

Yes, you do! But it's not an "either/or." It's an "and." Over the course of 15 years as a career coach, I've discovered that the best careers are about both money and meaning.

So how can you make all the money you want doing something you find personally fulfilling?

This is what you're about to learn in this book.

In these pages, you will learn how to open yourself up to what you were put here to do. (It's not just some of us who were put here to accomplish important things—it's all of us. And we weren't meant to suffer financially in order to do it.)

You will learn how to approach the job market in a fun and effective way

And you will learn how to ensure yourself the job security you crave

I love the "Plant Yourself Where You Will Bloom" approach because I know that in using it, your life will never be the same.

You will love what you're doing each and every day. You will know how to create long-term security for yourself. You will feel you are making a real contribution to the world. You'll stress less, get healthier, and have stronger relationships.

Sound good? I hope so! We'll be exploring all of this in depth, but for now, let's keep it simple by saying:

The difference between the old style of career choice and the new is that you flip the order of questions you ask yourself. Instead of asking what you can do to make money, you figure out what you want to do and then ask what it takes to make money at it.

This is what makes "Plant yourself where you will bloom" so powerful and will have you realizing the personal fulfillment and financial reward for which you long.

# CHAPTER 2

## Why You Need to

## "Plant Yourself Where You Will Bloom"

Over the course of a 40-year career, you are likely to spend 100,000 hours of your life working. That's one hundred thousand hours.

Just saying that, I almost feel as though I don't need to write anything else about why you need to "plant yourself where you will bloom."

But just in case, now that you have that statistic front and center, here are some things to ponder...

The hours you spend working will largely dictate whether or not you find it easy to be a happy person.

They'll have an impact on your health. They'll have an impact on your relationships. They'll have an impact on your finances.

Those 100,000 hours will have an impact on the world.

Every year, I talk with hundreds of women about their career hopes and dreams. The one thing I hear more often than anything else? "I just want to make a difference."

They don't even realize they're not being completely honest.

They don't just want to make a difference—they're already doing that. Everything they do has an impact; it makes a difference in the world. The problem is that they're not making a difference that matters to them.

Often when I'm working with a client, and she has pinpointed her perfect work, I ask her, "How happy would it make you to impact the world in this particular way?"

To a woman, a smile slowly spreads across her face, tears well up in her eyes, and she struggles to find the words to express her feelings.

No matter whether it's…

…Making life better for senior citizens, children, or animals…or taking patches of earth and transforming them from barren fields to community gardens…or helping people make their homes more energy efficient… or bringing families closer together in this hectic day and age…or helping athletes reach their peak performance…or helping people laugh in difficult times…

…Making the difference you want to make will make all the difference in your happiness.

\*\*\*\*\*\*\*\*\*\*\*\*\*\*\*\*

Would you say you're someone who lives to work or works to live?

Most of the women that I coach find themselves in the camp of working to live. They want to have rich, full, and joyful lives filled with family, friends, and fun activities. Work is just a part of the picture—not the whole enchilada. They're simply not willing to sacrifice enjoying the other important aspects of their life in the name of making money. Don't get me wrong—money is important to them and being able to meet all of their responsibilities is crucial—but it's not the only bottom line.

Life/Work Balance is extremely important for many of us. Unfortunately, there isn't just one magic formula. Which means it's often hard to achieve—especially given the necessity for the corporate world to maintain order by instituting standard employee policies.

And what is the result?

Stress-related illnesses such as chronic fatigue. Failed marriages. Strained parent-child relationships. Weight gain. Depression. Anxiety. Financial trouble.

Big sigh.

If you are experiencing any of these problems, there's hope. You're reading the right book.

Here are some of the results my clients have reported once they've planted themselves where they can bloom:

"I no longer have that knot in my stomach that I thought would never go away!"

"I've started enjoying my hobbies again—my photography is better than ever."

"I'm engaged!"

"I'm living a healthy life. I'm happy in my relationships. I'm happy and strong with myself. I'm able to contribute to the world. I feel totally engaged in life."

"I finally bought a house."

"I've released my excess weight and you will often find me in my art studio, expressing my artistic talents to my heart's content! I once again treasure my time with friends and family and have a clear plan to get my financial life back in the mode of prosperity."

\*\*\*\*\*\*\*\*\*\*\*\*\*\*\*\*\*\*

It's your choice how you will spend those 100,000 hours of your life—and thus you are also <u>choosing the ripple effect that you will create in your own life and in the world.</u>

If you see the need to plant yourself where you will bloom, keep reading…

# CHAPTER 3

## Why the Old Career Approach
## Won't Work for You

I have good news for you.

It's hardly a big secret: The world of work is changing rapidly. And truthfully, it's not just the world of work, but also the entire world that's changed.

Think about it: just 15 years ago, the Internet was an unknown quantity to most of us. Today, many of us organize our work-life—in fact, our life in general—around this ubiquitous, invisible behemoth.

Couple this with the fact that we are becoming far more globally-oriented than locally-minded, and you can see that the old adage, "Adapt or Die!" may be more imperative than ever.

And this is all great news!

Never before has it been so important, or in some ways easier, to make the difference that you most want to make in the world.

Why? Because whenever there's a major upheaval, there is chaos and fear and overwhelm. New problems develop that have to be solved. And that's where you come into the picture…since you are a unique blend of talents, interests, and values (and many other important things) you have the power to solve those problems. You have the opportunity to give your unique gift to the world.

\*\*\*\*\*\*\*\*\*\*\*\*\*\*\*\*\*

It only stands to reason that if the world of work is changing, you have to be willing to change along with it.

You can't win a new game playing by the old rules!

Time and again, as I'm teaching, I hear the frustration and desperation of talented people who simply can't find a job playing by the old rules of job searching. Wallpapering the town with dozens of resumes yields few, if any, actual job interviews.

It's not that work isn't out there. It's that the old system of cattle-call resume drives based on stale job descriptions simply doesn't meet the need for specialized employees. Instead of encouraging people to stand out and really shine, the system forces people (as one of my clients so aptly describes it) to fit into uncomfortable boxes with no holes for air.

When you see the need to plant yourself where you will bloom, you might also see that you are not just any flowering plant. You are probably an African Violet. Many of my clients are.

Do you know much about African Violets? The fact is they are one of the pickiest flowering plants in the world. Without exposure to just the right light (my mother swore by a western exposure), without putting the pot in a saucer with pebbles to keep the roots from getting too saturated, and without special fertilizer, they will never bloom.

If you are an African Violet, using traditional job search tactics will create the same effect in your life.

\*\*\*\*\*\*\*\*\*\*\*\*\*\*\*\*\*

In case you need convincing, let's illustrate just how ineffective the old approach to career choice and job search really is.

Get ready, because I'm about to take down the time-honored application tool known as "your resume."

Take a moment to think back over your career.

No matter how long or short it's been, would you say that you've been actively engaged in doing the best you could no matter the circumstances? Would you even say that at times you've put your whole heart and soul into it? In other words, have you been trying really hard to bloom where you are planted?

I bet you would.

Would you also say that your resume does a great job of showing this?

I bet not...

Resumes are simply not designed to highlight your heart and soul and dedication to your work.

Let's face it, your resume is a white piece of paper with black squiggles on it. Just like everyone else's resume. And, disturbingly, similar to a can of generic dog food.

It's not your fault. You're doing everything you can to get your resume right. You've looked up the advice of the professionals. You've run it past your family and friends. You really are taking your best shot at summing up your experience by following the rules of the game.

And therein lies the trouble. You're following all the rules of the old game, and it has turned you into a lemming.

Yes, I really did just say that it has turned you (really, all jobseekers) into lemmings.

Here's the problem with allowing this to happen...

What's the legend and lore of lemmings? Most of us associate them with a herd mentality—and you've probably seen images of them stampeding recklessly toward the edge of a cliff and senselessly plunging to their death in the raging ocean waters below.

Don't get me wrong—I have nothing against lemmings. They're cute, actually. A bit of a cross between a groundhog and a mouse.

The trouble with lemmings is that they all look alike. I doubt you could tell one from another unless you got to know them extremely well.

There's more trouble with being like a lemming, beyond even the generic nature of resumes. And I'm sure that you really don't want to run your career in a lemming-esque mode.

So let's look at some of the compelling reasons to avoid your resume making you act like a lemming in your career/job search.

**Lemmings look silly in blue suits**

If you saw a herd of lemmings dressed in little blue suits running toward a cliff, would it make a difference? Would it somehow make more sense of their behavior?

No! So it stands to reason that when we dress exactly like every other job hunter, all professional in our blue suit and sensible pumps, we are also subject to behaving exactly like every other job candidate who's being interviewed. That's the plight of the resume-led job search. In the interview, we fail to look, say, or do anything that distinguishes us from the rest of the herd. In fact, we can also begin to fear that there may not be anything all that special about us, after all.

## Lemmings have fluctuating populations

No one's really been able to document a reason for the lemmings' fluctuating populations. For our purposes, though, it bears giving some thought to the efficacy of "the next hot job trend" as a strategy for finding employment.

I teach a class that is designed to inform students of the latest employment trends and the up-and-coming small and large companies in Portland, OR.

Each term, I dutifully bring pages of data culled from various websites that cite the latest employment news.

A funny thing happens about 1/3 of the way into the class. The students begin to realize that they have no interest in, or affinity with, the growing industries.

Hallelujah!

I like to visualize my students instantly breaking free from the throngs of career-seekers who bet their future happiness on something as arbitrary as a need for more health-care workers to provide services to the aging baby-boomer population.

Because whenever enough people flock to a particular profession, the market becomes flooded with qualified applicants and suddenly the hot new career is now a bust.

And it's back to the drawing board, which looks a lot like another misdirected career change.

**Lemmings are suicidal**

Actually, this one is a myth. The reason the lemmings so earnestly flock is not that they can't find a reason to continue in this mad, mad, mad world.

It actually goes back to the issue of population.

When the competition for food and other necessities gets too intense, the lemmings pack up and migrate. Sometimes this migration requires the lemmings to swim across large bodies of water. As nature would have it, many of them are not strong enough to survive the swim.

Competition for job openings is not so different. Unlike the lemmings, though, we tend to stick with the process too long to save ourselves from the tyranny of lengthy unemployment. Rather than take the initiative to forge our way into a new career that's a better fit, we stay and duke it out in dying industries—just because we have the right career history.

**Lemmings fall from the sky**

That's what people used to believe.

A natural historian named Ole Worm (yes, that's his real name!) even believed that lemmings were brought by the wind.

I've met people who believe that the right job will fall from the sky and magically land in their lap. Like a lemming. Rather than take intentional action, they pray for a miracle.

It doesn't make much sense to wish for something and not take the steps to make it happen.

**Goodbye, Lemmings!**

When you're forging a path toward a new, vibrant, fulfilling career, the last thing you want to do is seem generic.

If your resume isn't able to show that you've been putting your heart and soul into your work; if it doesn't show that you are a unique and highly-capable person; if it makes you look just like every other job-seeker on the market…or worse…if it makes you doubt yourself and act as if you're nothing special…

Then your only logical choice is to compost your resume and vow to stop letting it make you act like a lemming.

*******************

Clearly, the old way of choosing a career and searching for a job is a system that needs to be fixed. Who can fix it? You can!

You can find a way to stand out and shine all on your own…

You can take a stand for doing impressive work through using your talents and living up to your personal values…

You can do a great job of getting noticed…

You can do a stellar job of staying connected to like-minded, inspiring people…

You can stop playing by (and losing the game with) the old rules and switch to what's really working for smart African Violets like you and me.

# CHAPTER 4

## An Overview of The
## "Plant Yourself Where You Will Bloom"
## Approach

You are about to embark on an exciting adventure…one that will continue to pay off in so many ways for years to come.

When you learn and apply the 7 steps of the "Plant Yourself Where You Will Bloom" career model, you write yourself a ticket to freedom.

The goal of this book is three-fold:

To teach you the elements of a smart strategy for discovering and making the leap to your perfect-fit work so that you are personally fulfilled and financially rewarded.

To reveal the best way to create your own job security—no matter what happens to any company or industry with which you are associated.

To get you jump-started on the path to the work you were born to do.

By learning and taking action on these ideas, you will experience:

- Getting into a better line of work that is joyful, rewarding, and fulfilling
  - Your personal relationships becoming easier
  - Making more money
  - Less stress

- A life with greater balance
- Ease with making decisions about things like moving, selling a house, having children
- More security in your financial future

Sounds pretty good, doesn't it?

\*\*\*\*\*\*\*\*\*\*\*\*\*\*\*\*\*

So what are the 7 steps of the "Plant Yourself Where You Will Bloom" Career Model? We'll be discussing them in depth in the following chapters, but let's take a moment for a brief overview:

### Step #1: Get a Crystal Clear Career Direction

The first step to planting yourself where you will bloom is to discover what makes you unique, so that you can turn it into a career direction that's both personally meaningful and financially rewarding. In this section, you will get an overview of the 8 key areas you need to explore about yourself and how to play with that information so that it points you to the right career path.

### Step #2: Explore the New World of Work

Suffice it to say, there's a great big world of work out there. And with all the rapid changes in technology (read: the internet) the world of work is growing exponentially.

Never has there been a better time to discover or invent the perfect work for you. In this section we'll show you how to explore what's new and exciting out there and how a good dose of creativity and imagination can help you leverage this information into a great job.

### Step #3: Get Connected to the Right People

There's just no substitute for knowing the right people at the right time.

But I'm not a big fan of most of the activities that are associated with traditional business networking. I have done very little of it in my career, and I heartily encourage you to abandon this activity and trade up to an exciting and much more sustainable approach.

In this section we'll discuss how to meet and nurture relationships with the people who will not only cheer when you cross the finish line with a great new career, but are the reason you're in the race in the first place.

### Step #4: Create and Build Your Community

Once you begin the process of meeting the right people, it's important to maintain your contacts as lifetime connections.

Rest assured—I'm not talking about creating an artificial, contrived way to stay in touch (that's almost as impersonal as traditional networking!)

In this section you'll learn about developing an exciting reason to share information and discoveries. I'm talking about linking together your "tribe" of industry people in a way that stimulates their creativity and challenges them to continue growing in the field, too.

**Step #5: Decide How to Make Money**

Yes, it's really your decision as to how you will make money—no matter what field you choose next. If you're used to settling for less than what you know you want to be earning, it's time to make adjustments.

In this section, we'll talk about the most practical matters associated with finances and career management. Adjusting your career never requires financial irresponsibility; in fact, it's quite the opposite. You'll learn a new way of looking at your financial needs and about the power of understanding business models.

**Step #6: Strategize Your Transition**

In this section, we'll get practical and rational about how you will transition into your perfect work. It's all about creating the ideal strategy for your particular situation.

You'll learn about the four modes of work and how they impact the job choices you'll make in moving forward.

**Step #7: Take Charge of Your Career**

As was mentioned earlier, the world of work is changing incredibly quickly and seemingly unpredictably. So what's the best way for you to create lifelong job security?

Even after you're in your perfect work you can't run things on autopilot and expect that everything will be just fine. And you can't just think about your career when your current job is about to (or has already) ended.

In this section you'll learn how to take an active approach to nurturing your career and providing yourself the kind of job security most people only dream about.

*****************

Whenever you make an investment in your career, you are ensuring that you will stay ahead of the trends and possibilities—something that more than 80% of the population never chooses. This means that you can be one of the few who never have to worry where their next paycheck is coming from.

So go ahead—pat yourself on the back for taking the initiative!

Notice that I said investment? Any time you make an investment, you're hoping for dividends. There's a lot that you could receive from this book… a new perspective about the world of work and where you fit, the inspiration for a new career direction, and a strategy for taking action.

Notice that I said could receive?

What, no guarantees?

Yep! No guarantees! At least, not from me, even though I know that this approach has worked time and again for my clients.

Here's why:

The only guarantee can come from you. If you read this book with an open mind and heart, you will see the results you're looking for. I can't make you read it—and I can't make you have an open mind and heart. It's completely up to you.

I'm here to guide you along the way, and I consider it an honor and a privilege. I plan to share with you information that you can immediately begin using in your own career. You'll hear the real-life stories of my most successful clients. So please—take the inspiration when you find it and use it to your best advantage.

# CHAPTER 5

## How the "Plant Yourself Where You Will Bloom" Approach Changed My Life

I often get asked about whether or not I've used this approach in my own career. If you're curious as well, here's my story:

I like to tell people that I "escaped professional misery" about twelve years into my career.

Believe me, it was a long and painful journey getting there.

After graduating from college, I struggled to find a professional job. Eventually, through a temporary help service, I landed in a giant of a high tech company.

I rose through the ranks to a great job as a sales representative in high tech, making good money, but I wasn't happy. I had no interest in the products I was selling (and truthfully, I didn't even understand them completely!). I never felt comfortable doing the things that were required for me to be successful. My boss was more interested in seeing my sales numbers than in seeing my face. So, thinking it might be just the company I worked for, I tried the same job in another company. And naturally, the situation wasn't any better. So I tried again, and got the same results! Something just wasn't working here…

Finally the day came when my heart broke wide open. I was about to take another job in high tech. My prospective boss told me it was perfect for me and I'd be crazy not to take it. Seeing no other choice, I accepted her offer.

I hung up the phone and sat on the edge of my bed for a minute. Then I collapsed to the floor, closed my eyes, and tried to stop my mind from spinning. I heard an eerie sound that frightened me because I'd never heard anything like it. I now know it was the sound of keening—a low, guttural moan often heard when people mourn.

The sound was coming from me.

In my heart of hearts, I knew that I was sacrificing my happiness yet again. I knew this new job would not be a situation in which I could bloom. I would not be using my greatest talents. I simply was not interested in the service I would be selling. I did not value the difference I would be making in the world by doing this work. I felt compromised on all levels by making this career move.

What was most unfortunate was that I didn't feel I had many options. I did not yet know where to plant myself so that I would bloom.

So I decided to take the job because I needed the money, but I also vowed to get the support I needed to discover a career that would work for me. I hired a career consultant, which is one of the best moves I've made in my life.

In a very short while…Nirvana!

I was able to get a clear direction for work that would be ideal for me. I wanted to help people avoid the same professional struggle I had faced. After a little while of tweaking things, I discovered career coaching and knew immediately it was exactly what I'd been looking for.

I was fascinated with the kinds of discussions my work required. I was thrilled I could work from home, since that was the perfect situation given that I was the mother of two young children. I loved the training as it completely fed my curiosity. I was overjoyed at how the freedom of creating a business from scratch matched my independent nature.

In a very short time, I went from dreading Monday mornings to feeling as though my professional life was effortless and fascinating.

It's been 15 years, and every day I can honestly say that I'm happy in my work. Thus, I want the same thing for you. I just don't want it to take you as long as it took me. And that's why I've written this for you. And that's why I run workshops and provide lots of other tools to help people just like you escape your version of professional misery. If I could do it—I know you can, too.

*****************

These 7 steps are a complete system for creating and developing your career.

Each step is designed with a very special objective in mind: to rescue you from the disheartening experiences inherent in the old career search model. Oh, and one more thing…

…To help you make the world a better place by giving your unique gift.

You may be thinking that it's pretty lofty to consider yourself one of the people who are going to solve the world's problems.

I'm here to tell you it's not lofty at all. Because if it's not you who's going to do it, who is? The other people reading this book? Well, I certainly hope they are, too! I hope each and every one of you is here because you want to make a significant contribution to making the world a better place.

Simply put, I believe that the world will be a great place when everyone does work they love. Can you imagine it? It won't happen if only some of us are willing, but what if everyone reading this book made the commitment?

Let's talk a bit about how this can be so much easier than it sounds, so you can let yourself envision your success, no matter what.

******************

Nowadays, it's easy to hang out in the thought realm that everything is a big struggle, competition is fierce, no one is hiring, and the economy is ridiculously slow in recovering.

The key phrase in there is "thought realm." You may have skimmed right over this phrase, but it's an important concept, and one that will inform how you use the information in this book.

Whether you realize it or not, you choose what you think about. You decide upon what you will focus.

The world can be viewed in two ways: as a place of lack or as a place of abundance.

You can think about what's wrong with the world of work and why you can't succeed, or you can look for where you fit best and begin to thrive.

You can see all the obstacles to making things happen and quit, or you can see the clues hidden within what seem to be problems and press forward.

You can play the career game the same way everyone else is playing it, or you can choose a path that's custom-made for you and your goals.

You can view yourself as a talented and dedicated individual, or as a member of a faceless and hopeless crowd.

Isn't this the best news of all? That your career success is entirely up to you and how you choose to view things?

I thought so.

# PART I

# CAREER EPIPHANY:

## *Discover Your Perfect Work*

# CHAPTER 6

## Cultivating Seeds of Greatness

**Step #1: Get a Crystal Clear Career Direction**

"Getting to know you. Getting to know all about you…"

-- Oscar Hammerstein, lyrics from *The King and I*

Pop Quiz!

I know—can you believe it? You've barely started reading the book and I'm giving you a pop quiz. Don't be nervous. Your grade will not be going on your permanent record! Besides, if you reread step number one as written on this page, you'll know the answer…

Here goes:

Every term at Portland Community College I teach a class called, "Who Do You Think You Are?"

I always hand out a questionnaire that asks, "What do you hope to get from this class?"

What do you think is the #1 most frequent answer students give?

That's right! They're looking for a direction for their career.

That wasn't so hard, was it?

Finding a direction for your career can definitely seem hard at first, too. What it requires is that you do the necessary introspective work to discover what kind of flower you are so that you can plant yourself where you will bloom. Remember, if you're an African Violet like most of my clients, you won't be happy just anywhere. If you're a dandelion, well, a crack in just about any sidewalk will do.

In this chapter, you'll learn how, just like a plant's DNA determines what kind of flower it produces, certain aspects of what makes you unique can be combined to show you where you will bloom.

******************

When you first got started, what did you think your career was going to look like?

From your current vantage point of 20/20 hindsight…would you say that before you jumped into the world of work you spent a lot of time thinking about what would be the perfect work for you?

Or is it possible that you started with a basic idea of what might be good, and then quickly found yourself reacting to opportunities—and quite possibly making choices based on the need for money?

Well, if so, no worries. It's a story I hear a lot. The trouble with this approach is that it's hard to stop reacting to opportunities. Like the Titanic, it's hard to turn that ship around and lead the way to taking strategic steps. So what happens is that you get a little more off course with each job change. Eventually, the work you're doing bears little resemblance to anything that leverages your core talents, values, and interests.

And then you hit the iceberg. The stress levels go off the charts. You start getting headaches that mushroom into migraines. You feel like no matter what you do, you can't get ahead. People are depending on you. Expectations are high. You struggle to deliver. Maybe you start pushing against the system. Vacations are a thing of the past. You can't quite figure out why you're making money but don't seem to be saving…and it goes on.

Everyone's story is a little different, but you get the gist. It all adds up to disappointment, disillusionment, and the feeling you just aren't making the kind of contribution you want to be making.

At this point, you're way off course from your perfect work. But you don't have to stay that way! You really can have it all—once you know what "it all" really is…

## Defining Perfect Work

Before we get too far, it's probably a good idea to address the possibility that you are reacting to the word "perfect." It's the kind of word that triggers strong emotions in people. You might be in the camp of "nothing's perfect." Or the camp of "everything's perfect." Or you might be a "perfectionist" who gets frustrated by trying to achieve the unattainable.

Letting go of all these hang-ups means that we can look at what's essential in this picture:

Your perfect work is the set of circumstances in which the best of you can shine.

Being in your perfect work doesn't mean that every day is full of sunshine, warm chocolate chip cookies, and puppy breath. It doesn't mean you won't face challenges. It doesn't mean there won't be the occasional failure along with your successes. It's not a guarantee that all your worries are over (the only way to guarantee that is to completely shift your attitude and become someone who simply sees the value in everything that happens—thus…no worries!)

If it's not these things…then what is being in your perfect work? Well, there are three parts to this equation: Love your work; work with love; work with your life. Let's look at them one at a time…

**Love Your Work**

What do you actually spend your time doing on a daily basis? What activities are you engaging in? Do you enjoy the skills you're developing? Are you leveraging your "core competency"—the thing you do better than anything else?

All these questions have a bottom line…they reflect your talents.

Talents

Talents are those things that you do effortlessly and easily. You were born with a natural ability and you truly enjoy using the talent and developing it. For many people (including me) it makes sense to orient your new career around your greatest talent. If you regularly get to do what you do best, you will find your career satisfaction going through the roof!

But talent isn't the only important element of perfect work…

Another crucial aspect is whether you feel truly connected to your industry. Do you care about the purpose of your current organization? For instance, if your job is selling shoes, do you feel a sense of connection to the importance of shoes in this world? Do you like thinking about shoes? Do you enjoy testing out the new products and talking to people about the unique features and benefits of every pair?

These questions also have a bottom-line…they reflect your interests.

Interests

So what captivates your attention? What do you enjoy thinking about? Are you fascinated by something? Do you feel passionate about a particular cause? Is there a wrong you'd like to see made right in the world?

Having a sincere interest in what your work is about can make a significant difference in your sense of fulfillment. I frequently ask students in my classes, "Is it worth doing if it's not interesting?"

How do you answer that question? Are you committed to doing work that you find really interesting?

You can often detect your interests by reflecting on the various types of informal education in which you've engaged. Community education classes, books, and online communities can all point the way to your biggest areas of interest. And every interest has an industry associated with it. And every industry has businesses in need of passionate employees.

Talents and interests are two pieces of the "love your work" puzzle— but there's one more…

In this case, it's what you know, not who you know! Are you utilizing your area of expertise? Do you have specialized knowledge or skills that you would love to be using? Have you shied away from making use of your formal training?

The answers to these questions reflect your base of knowledge.

Knowledge

Whereas interests are all about your informal education, knowledge reflects the formal aspect. If you've received a degree (or degrees), certificates, licensing, or on-the-job training, you have specialized knowledge.

**Work With Love**

Chances are good you've caught yourself thinking about loving your work, but have you ever thought about yourself working with love?

This is not a common term so don't worry about it. I bet we can find some other word you've used that reflects the essence of this phrase. How about integrity? Are you someone who shows, or wants to show, a great deal of integrity in your work?

If so, have you thought about where your integrity comes from? The shortcut answer is…your values.

Values

Let's be clear. When I refer to values, I'm not talking about morals or ethics. While those are important to have, too, values are the king of the hill when it comes to doing your work in a way that is full of integrity—and, yes, loving.

Values are those things that you find most valuable in life. Where do you find value in your life? Family? Fun? Friends? Creativity? Beauty? Leadership? The list is long.

When you orient your work around the things that you find valuable, you will naturally be drawn to performing your job in a way that is consistent with the noblest part of who you are. As a result, you will have greater respect for yourself. The added bonus is that the people you work with and for will see that self-respect and treat you with respect as well.

**Work With Your Life**

I once took a career assessment that advised me to consider orienting my career choice around my lifestyle.

What? I was flabbergasted. I thought this was incredibly shallow. For me, it seemed to mean that how I wanted to live my life was more important than the contribution I wanted to make. It felt materialistic, soul-less, and, dare I say it? Self-Centered.

It took a while for the real truth of this to sink in. And it has actually ended up guiding my career choices—but not in the way that I expected.

I realized that, yes, I cared about my whole life, not just my career. Yes, I had goals set in other areas beyond my work. Yes, it mattered to me how many hours I worked each day. Yes, it mattered to me what my work environment was like, and whom the people were that I was working with and for.

The truth revealed by all of this was (and is) that I have distinct preferences. And you do, too.

Preferences

What would the world be like if people didn't have preferences? Think about Coke vs. Pepsi. McDonalds vs. Burger King. Spandex vs. Cotton. Without preferences, the world would be a pretty boring place.

Preferences are what make specific jobs perfectly fit specific people. Whether you realize it or not, you really do have an opinion about who you love to work with—those are your co-workers. You care about who you work for—that would be your boss. And you care about who you serve – your customers.

You care about how much or how little money you make.

You also care a little or a lot about your work environment, and a whole slew of other lifestyle choices. You probably have certain hours of the day that you would prefer to work, as well as how many hours each day. You prefer working in certain types of clothing. You prefer a way of getting to work and how long it takes you. The list is practically endless.

And in the end, it will all add up to working with your life. Because your life is about more than work—it's about respecting things like community, family, finances, romance, and contribution.

Yes, this is where we're talking about Life/Work Balance. As an African Violet, you likely want to have a rich, full, and joyful life filled with family, friends, and fun activities. Work is just a part of the picture—not the whole picture. Knowing this will make all the difference in your ability to identify the perfect work scenario when you see it.

And therein was my personal ah-ha about orienting my career around lifestyle. When I first became a career consultant, I was dissatisfied and had to figure out why. I realized that when I was consulting, the client focus was simply on careers. We weren't taking into consideration how the career fit within the client's whole life. Then I found life coaching and realized that it was a much better fit for me to work with people more holistically, taking into account everything that matters in their world. Gotta love those career epiphanies!

**Your Personal Perfect Work Status**

Chances are good that you haven't taken the time to assess your personal knowledge of yourself in each of the 8 key areas: talents, interests, values, knowledge, and preferences regarding money, people, environment, and lifestyle.

On the following page is a tool to help you assess just how much you know about yourself in each of these areas.

Here are the instructions:

1. Review each of the 8 areas of the career wheel.

2. For each area, rate yourself on a scale of 1-10 (with 1 being "not at all true" and 10 being "totally true") by answering these questions:

Rating _____ I know all of my talents.

Rating _____ I know all of my interests.

Rating _____ I know all of my values.

Rating _____ I can name my areas of formal and informal knowledge.

Rating _____ I know my preferences regarding making money.

Rating _____ I know my preferences regarding the people I work with, work for, and work to help.

Rating _____ I know what environment brings out my best.

Rating _____ I know what I want to honor regarding my lifestyle preferences.

3. Now, put a dot in the ring that corresponds with your rating, within each area of the career wheel.

4. Now connect the dots.

If this were a wheel on a car, how bumpy would your ride be? You can probably see now why it is that your career so far has been such an uncomfortable journey! If you are not a "10" in each of those areas, you are likely headed in the wrong direction.

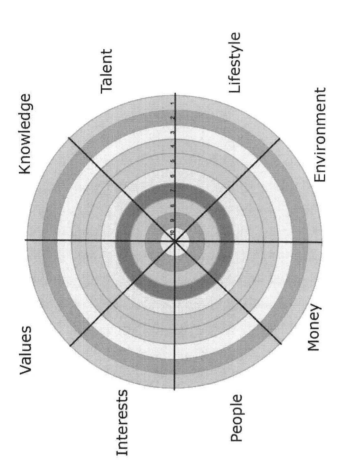

Adapted by Jennifer Anderson & Kent Blumberg from Whitworth, L., Kimsey-House, K., Kimsey-House, H., & Sandahl, P. (2007). *Co-active coaching: New skills for coaching people toward success in work and life.* Mountain View, CA: Davies-Black Publishing

## The Sweet Spot

If you like sports, you might know what this term means. It's used to describe the specific spot on a racket or club or bat where the force is completely balanced. Hit the ball in the sweet spot and watch it soar to your desired destination.

Careers have a sweet spot, too! It's the exact center of the career wheel (the "10" rating) where the eight elements of the career wheel converge.

The sweet spot is the combination of information that comprises the ideal solution. If any one of the career elements gets overlooked so that info is missing, you won't have a complete picture.

This means you will make a choice based on incomplete information. Which means you might find yourself going down another dead-end road.

We don't want that to happen ever again!

It's important to go the distance to discover as much information about yourself as possible in each of the eight areas.

## Cooking Up A Sweet Spot

I always like to have an example of a concept to really bring home the point. So let's take a minute to create the perfect work for a pretend client:

**Meet Sally…**

Sally is 38 years old and is a talented cook. Several years ago she attended culinary school, but never did much with it. Now she's ready to get into the workforce and is exploring her opportunities to use her talent for cooking.

What are some of Sally's options? She could…

Cook for an elementary school cafeteria

Cook in a fast food restaurant

Cook in a Chinese restaurant

Be a personal chef

…And probably dozens more places.

But what happens if we add in just one more of the elements of the career wheel?

Let's say that Sally has a fascination with cooking gourmet French food. How long would Sally be happy in any of the above cooking environments? Not long!

It's easy to see that she could take just any old cooking job, thereby using her talent, but by doing so she would not be exploring her interest and would end up suffering in her job.

Let's take it another step further, and fill in some more information:

Talent = Cooking

Interest = Gourmet French Food

Value = Health

Knowledge = Culinary Institute Training

Preferences = Slower pace, the opportunity to try and refine new recipes, regular 9-5 work hours, work from home.

Now what might be the perfect work for Sally?

Maybe catering, with a specialty in healthy gourmet French food. Maybe as a test cook for a French gourmet health food website. What else can you think of?

In any case, hopefully it's now a lot easier to see how important it is to go the distance—to get all the information about yourself that you possibly can so that you will instantly recognize the perfect opportunity for yourself!

## The Orienting Factor

While there are eight distinct areas for exploration, and each is important, they aren't necessarily equally important.

Most of my clients have discovered that one of the eight areas tends to be a bit more important than the others. In other words, it becomes the central orienting factor—the one thing that cannot be compromised.

For my client Ryan, "people" are the central orienting factor. As he made his way through my Career Epiphany coaching program, we noticed that no matter the topic of exploration for the week, he eventually brought the discussion back to people. He saw very clearly that the people he worked with (his peers), the people he worked for (his bosses), and the people he served (his clients) mattered more to him than anything else.

For you it could be values, or a passionate interest, or a preference for a particular set of lifestyle standards.

The good news is that while you're exploring and gathering information about yourself, your orienting factor usually becomes pretty obvious. So embrace it and run with it! It's all good...

*****************

Clearly, the first step to planting yourself where you will bloom is to discover what makes you unique. When you gather as much information about yourself as possible in each of the 8 pieces of the career wheel, you can then look for that perfect intersection—your very own sweet spot!

It's no small accomplishment. I know—because helping people do this is what I've dedicated my career to for the last 15 years. And I guarantee that if you'll take the time for this big adventure, you'll find yourself in the happiest of places—loving your work, working with love, and working with your life.

\*\*\*

**Ready to begin discovering your perfect work?**

**Go to www.Start2Bloom.com**

\*\*\*

# Shannon's Story

## Embrace Who You Are
## and Change the Entire Course of Your History

What do you do when you're tired of putting up with nonsense? When every fiber of your being is screaming out that you can no longer continue doing the same things and expecting different results?

Meet Shannon. Bright, attractive, vivacious, and honest.

At age 40, Shannon is simply no longer willing to ignore that the first 40 years of her life were not much fun. She is determined to make sure that she truly enjoys her next 40 years (or more!)

When Shannon became my client, she realized that she couldn't make herself "do just anything" anymore. She felt that when she was younger she could make herself do whatever she needed to do to make money. But now, she found herself in what she describes as "increasing revolt."

She clearly saw that she needed to get her career in alignment with who she is.

### Shannon's Path toward Self-Discovery

Recently, I asked Shannon to describe her experience of working with me to discover her perfect work. Her answer?

"Extremely enlightening. It's a relief for one thing, to know that who I am, contrary to what I've been told, is OK. I don't need to fit into this mold that was set out for me…because it wasn't fitting!"

Shannon is right—how you are and who you are is absolutely perfect and wonderful. And there's definitely a fit in the world of work…for her—and for you.

### Shannon's Career Epiphany

Shannon was a bit surprised to discover that the right path has been speaking to her for a very long time.

"I'm treading in not completely foreign territory. My mind has made a lot of these things clear over the years, and I was to some degree already moving in (this direction)."

This is not an unusual phenomenon. Taking the time to do your self-exploration usually provides you with the necessary evidence and information that fills in the blanks so that you can fully embrace what's right for you.

### Shannon's Advice

"Change is such a difficult process; even when you're willing, it's really difficult. And, Lord knows, I've been willing!

"I found this quote that really helped me process change:

'The most important thing to remember is this: to be ready at any moment to give up what you are for what you might become.' W.E.B. Dubois.

"This quote helps remind you that you're trying to make a change for a purpose, and that purpose is going to require you to give up some of the things that you believe or have done prior to that purpose.

"Each little step makes you stronger in doing the next step."

**What's Next for Shannon?**

"It's going to be an exciting new year, is what it's going to be. This is going to help me change the entire course of my history. And I'm really looking forward to that!"

***

**Want to hear more of Shannon's Story?  Listen to the audio of Shannon describing her career journey at**

**www.Start2Bloom.com**

***

# PART II

# CAREER EXPEDITION:

*Discover Your Next Right Job*

# CHAPTER 7

## *Searching for Fertile Ground*

**Step #2: Explore the New World of Work**

"Have no expectations of what you're going to find.

Just have a happy, expectant attitude

As if you were embarking on a treasure hunt."

-- Sarah Ban Breathnach

Remember when you were first learning to drive and the driver's ed movie talked about taking in "The Big Picture?" We were taught to scan the whole scene around us so that we wouldn't miss anything (and potentially get in an accident).

When you're driving, the last thing you want to wear are blinders. When you can only stare ahead, you miss everything off to the sides and even the stuff behind you!

Same goes for exploring the world of work.

Would it surprise you to know that you're probably aware of less than 20% of the career options in this great big world? It's pretty likely.

In the career search class I teach, each term I share a list of the best 100 companies to work for in Oregon. The students are always amazed to realize that they've only heard of about 20 of the companies. And these are the BEST one hundred companies in Oregon!

Suffice it to say, there's a great big world of work out there. And with all the rapid changes in technology (read: internet) the world of work is growing like a weed.

Never has there been a better time to discover or invent the perfect work for you. All it takes is a bit of awareness about what's new and exciting out there and then a good dose of creativity and imagination to see how to leverage this information.

We've all had those sudden moments of insight—often about things that aren't necessarily all that important. Looking for a discovery related to something as key as your work can be a bit more daunting.

Later in this chapter we'll reveal the best sources for up-to-date information, but first, a word about attitude.

*****************

Before you read any further, go back and read Sarah Ban Breathnach's advice in the quote that begins this chapter...

...Welcome back!

So how do you feel about going on this particular treasure hunt?

If you've had any trepidation about making a change in your career, it's understandable.

Most people have an awful lot invested in making the right career choice. After all, your decision can impact every major aspect of your life—your family, where you live, how much money you make, and your day-to-day experience of happiness.

With this much on the line, it's no wonder you can be a bit reluctant to take a lot of chances. It's easy to shut down and decide to play it safe.

So just exactly "who" do you need to be to open up to seeing this as a treasure hunt?

**Someone who is EXCITED**

Are you excited to go on this journey? Are you intensely curious as to what you'll discover? Do you feel like you're beyond ready and are willing to make some adjustments to the life you're leading? If so, you're in the right place! Onward ho!!

If you're not, then let me be honest. If you're in a desperate situation, and have to make an immediate change, this may not be the best time for you to take risks. Simply put, you're under too much pressure. You might have too much at stake to really open up to the possibilities. Only you can know for sure, but if you *need* to make a discovery, it's not a good sign. It's far better to create some stability in your life first—and then go for the gusto of a brand new direction.

**Someone who SEEKS inspiration**

Did you know that nothing happens in life without first being inspired? It's true. Everything you've ever accomplished has been the direct result of your being inspired to create or achieve it. Even the little things, like what you decide to have for breakfast, are inspired somehow. You might be inspired to eat eggs because they are a high quality protein and you are working to build stronger muscles. You might be inspired to have yogurt because you want calcium for stronger bones. You might be inspired to have chocolate cake because it…well, it makes you happy!

For our purposes, it's important for you to actively seek out inspiration. Become aware of the little things that catch your attention and discern the importance and meaning. Clues are all around you—and if you can embrace that truth and ask to be inspired, it will happen.

### Someone who is OPEN to new perspectives and universal truths

Ever feel like you're stuck in a rut? Of course you have; we've all felt that way many times in our lives. Rut states are created by a lack of new information—we keep thinking about things the same old way. Based on the same old input. It's like we're one of those wind-up toys that keeps bumping into the wall, gets thrown back a few inches, then marches forward again only to hit the wall and repeat the cycle.

Simply put, you won't get anywhere new by looking at things the same old way. The only solution is to actively seek new perspectives. And often that means talking to new people from different walks of life. You'll have to be willing to widen your circle of acquaintances and invite them to share their divergent beliefs and attitudes. This isn't to say that you have to accept their truths wholesale; rather, take in the new information, integrate it with what you already know, and see the brand new picture.

### Someone who is CURIOUS to know what's uniquely true about yourself

Snowflakes. Humans are just like snowflakes. No two are alike. No one in this world is exactly like you! It's easy to see why when you consider the fact that no one else has had your same set of opportunities and experiences.

Why does it matter whether you know the unique truth about yourself? Because the answer to the question of what is your perfect work is a blend of your values, talents, interests, knowledge, and preferences. You'll never be able to figure it out without this information.

It's not narcissistic or self-indulgent to want to know all about you—it's smart. If you believe you were put here for a reason, you'll be curious to know what it is that you've been given to pull it off.

## Someone who LISTENS to your HEART FIRST and then your MIND SECOND

It's no accident that we are born with both a mind and a heart—and I'm talking about something beyond the physical need for both these vital organs. Figuratively speaking, they serve distinctly different purposes for discovering and pursuing perfect work.

They're important at different stages of the process. It's important to get this straight! If you don't, you'll never make a new discovery...

Let your heart speak first. Your heart houses the truth about what you really want to be doing in this world. It's not always rational, so it doesn't always make sense. Your heart can lead you places that you never expected to go—places where you have amazing experiences that are all designed to equip you for what's coming next in life.

The heart is optimistic. It's the realm of vision and mission and purpose. It sees the potential and possibilities—the big stuff about what life could be like at its finest.

It can be pretty tough to let your heart have its say. Many of the world's cultures place a high premium on being rational and logical. We're trained to analyze the evidence and make a sound decision based on the likelihood of success. This is the realm of the mind.

Trouble is, the mind is fairly pessimistic. It's designed to protect us in the most primitive of ways. The mind is highly invested in the status quo—there's perceived safety in what's already known. (Notice I said "perceived" safety.)

The greatest advances in the sciences and the arts have created immense safety for humans. In fact, we live in a world where little is an actual threat to our imminent well-being. And those advances are a direct result of someone listening to their heart, being inspired, and taking action.

I did say, though, that the mind serves an important purpose in this process…

Once your heart has its say, that's the cue for the mind to come in and work its magic. The task is to answer one simple question: How do I make this happen?

**Someone who TRUSTS your gut**

Call it a gut feeling. Call it intuition. Call it that small, still voice inside you. Call it anything you want—just don't ignore it!

Each of us is born with an internal guidance system that constantly begs for our attention. Like the heart, it's not necessarily rational. It just seems to "know" the truth and what's right for us.

You might have noticed that when you pay attention to that little voice, you're often rewarded. And when you ignore it, things don't go so smoothly.

For our purposes, it's a great idea to get comfortable checking in with your gut feeling or intuition about things. Start to notice what that voice sounds or feels like. Many people experience it as being fairly calm, certain, and matter-of-fact.

This guidance is invaluable and it will pay off, over and over again, when you trust it.

### Someone who BELIEVES it will happen

Reality check. Are you optimistic or pessimistic? Do you believe this can happen? Do you believe this is the right time to accept this insight? Are you ready to take action? Do you trust that this will be an adventure? Do you trust that the other side of the wall will be a land of excitement, opportunity, rewards, and fulfillment?

Take some time now to assess your beliefs.

Even if you're not quite all the way to this attitude—do you somehow know that you're meant to go on this journey anyway?

### The Art of Research

Now that you know "who" you need to be, it's time to reveal "what" you need to do to explore the new world of work. Following are a few suggestions of valuable resources that act as good starting points. Don't be surprised if you've heard of all of them. But do be surprised to discover some new ways to utilize these resources.

## *Job Fairs*

I begin with this suggestion with a fair amount of trepidation.

I am of the opinion that a job fair is the absolute worst place to go to find an actual job. In all these years, I've never had anyone tell me that's how he or she got a job.

While they stink for actual employment, job fairs are a great place to do research. The companies present at the fair are like sitting ducks. They bring all their corporate literature and most of the time the poor booth attendants are desperate to have a conversation with someone interesting (read: you).

So go ahead—wander the showroom floor and grab as many contacts as you can. Pick up business cards and literature. Create a standard list of questions that you can ask anyone about his or her particular job, company, or industry. Take the time to see whether you resonate with the overall "feel" of the company's literature and approach.

Here's where I get a little bossy:

*Under no circumstances should you take a resume.* Trust me on this one! I'll explain more in the next chapter.


## *The Library*

Don't shut down on me now. If the mere mention of doing research at the library sends you tumbling back to dreadful days spent in high school and college library "stacks," just trust me; when you're not in school the library is an oasis, not a muck!

And your best friend at the library is most definitely the Reference Librarian. I tell you, these folks are like dogs with a bone when you give them a research question. They will lead you expeditiously through aisles of resources and pinpoint exactly what even you didn't know you were looking for.

I once had a magnificent Reference Librarian triumphantly chase me down in the parking lot because he had continued to search for a resource I needed—even after we'd finally given up.

Through your library, you will have free access to super expensive databases that house invaluable information for anyone wanting a better picture of the world of work.

Puzzled? Just ask your Reference Librarian to point you in the right direction!

### *Associations*

Did you know there is an association for absolutely every industry in the world of work?

It's true because the book that lists all the known associations is heavy enough to do some real damage if it were hurled at a Humvee. This magical book is the mastermind of the American Society of Association Executives. That's right—there's even an association for association executives!

An association, at a minimum, operates at a national or international level for most fields. Depending on the size of your town, you may also discover that there is a local chapter. If this is the case, be prepared to discover a smorgasbord of companies in your industry, and a bevy of wonderful contacts within those companies.

### *Alumni Centers*

If you've participated in post-secondary education of any kind, chances are good there's an alumni center for your school.

Most people approach these centers with the hope that they will help them find a job. Most of those people are sadly disappointed.

The great news is that although these centers are not oases of jobs, they are definitely oases of people who are working—and you just might discover the vastness of the world of work. Not to mention the tiny corner of the world that you fit into perfectly.

### LinkedIn

If you've been resisting the leap into Social Networking, now's a great time to reconsider.

I won't deny that it's easy to waste a lot of time on sites like Facebook and Twitter. But LinkedIn is a different story. As John, a good friend of mine, taught me: Facebook is for friends, Twitter is for strangers, and LinkedIn is for business.

In later chapters, we'll be talking more extensively about how to use LinkedIn to land yourself in your perfect job. But for now our focus is research, and here's how to use it for that:

When you are linked to someone on LinkedIn, did you know that not only are you able to view their information, you're also able to view the information of the people they know?

That's right! One of my clients told me that because just one of his colleagues was linked to him, he discovered that he could view the basic information of more than 1700 people!

Why does this matter? Well, a huge percentage of those 1700 people (remember—this is the statistic for just *one* contact) are actively involved in the world of work. By doing a little perusing, you will be able to discover industries and organizations that you never knew existed!

### *Local Publications*

Believe it or not, the classifieds are not just for lining birdcages anymore!

Although the "want ads" are definitely past their prime as a tool for getting a job, it's still a fairly decent hunting ground for discovering local companies.

Don't overlook the business pages of your local newspaper, either. They might house the latest information about local companies, information about the major and minor players in local business, and a listing of local business events that are open to the public to attend.

Your town might even have a Business Journal that comes out on a weekly basis. If that's the case, it's a good idea to subscribe or check it out online (if that's an option). The pages will be filled with stories about what's happening in your neck of the woods—including which companies are thriving and which companies are diving.

Another possibility is that your local Business Journal prints what they call "The List." Each week, "The List" focuses on a different aspect of business in your area. One week it might be the top 10 architect firms and the next it might be the highest-paid executives. At the end of each year, the journal prints its "Book of Lists," which houses the previous year's 52 weekly lists. As you can imagine, these are available for many, many previous years. It's a veritable treasure chest of information!

### *The Bus Stop*

Lest you think there isn't an old-fashioned way to go about doing this, never forget the power of striking up conversations any and everywhere you go!

Feel free to ask people what they know and who they know. You never know who you might be attracting just in time to point you in the right direction.

\*\*\*\*\*\*\*\*\*\*\*\*\*\*\*\*\*

Taking the time to explore and get to know the new world of work will undoubtedly pay off exponentially.

You'll want to prepare to be surprised by all kinds of synchronicities.

A few years ago, when my client Anissa had her career epiphany, she realized that she really did want to be an ultrasound technician. She had explored the field before, but discovered that no training programs existed where she lived. So she had abandoned this particular path.

After her epiphany pointed her in the same direction, Anissa stopped by her local community college and was amazed to discover that they were starting a new ultrasound program later that year!

She was accepted into and completed the program within a very short time.

To paraphrase Winston Churchill, "Never give up. In matters either great or small. Never give up."

Even if it seems you're not on the right path, take all the information you find and look for where you are being directed.

As they say, leave no stone unturned. And don't forget to explore your neighborhood. Sometimes the most fertile ground is found in your own backyard…keep reading to see what I mean!

# Kristi's Story

## Figuring Out What Sort of People
## Speak the Same Language I Do

What do you do when you're sure you're not doing the right work, but you haven't figured out in what direction you need to go? When you're looking for the light at the end of the tunnel, but all you see is darkness—no matter how hard you squint?

Meet Kristi. Sweet, sensitive, and intellectual. When she came to my series of career classes and then my weekend workshop, she'd been trying to solve her career puzzle for a long time, without success. She thought maybe she needed to really look at all the practical steps of the process to get herself going in the right career direction.

"I'm not exactly sure what I was hoping (to get from the classes)…I was looking for hope, basically."

### Kristi's Career Epiphany

Kristi decided to take the hint when a piece of information about her showed up in the results of more than one of the workshop exercises.

"Probably my biggest surprise was that aesthetics—the way things look—matters to me."

Kristi is fascinated by the architectural interior design of buildings—and has been for a long time.

In fact, during the workshop she recounted that one of her favorite places to spend time is in the lobby of a hotel in Tacoma, WA. She explained that the design is built around art glass. She loves it so much that her now-husband actually proposed to her in the lobby when he saw how thrilled she was to be there.

Kristi gets excited when she comes across a building that she didn't know existed—so much so that when she shares her excitement with friends, they can't help but tell her she's in the right place with her career.

### Kristi's Exploration of the New World of Work

Finding the right niche within this field has been a bit of a slower process for Kristi. She remains thoroughly committed to exploring all her options before jumping into a career decision too quickly.

"After taking your workshop, I found myself, within a couple of months, taking interior design classes at the local community college…I'm just remarkably interested in the subject matter. Now I'm two years into the design thing, and I'm completely fascinated.

I think if I could find a way to be a cheerleader, an informed cheer-leader, for people who are tackling (design) projects on their own—that (would be) really exciting."

Kristi recently had the opportunity to spend a few months in Copenhagen. Her husband is from Denmark, which she thinks is completely serendipitous.

"The whole design thing is incredibly tied in with that (Copenhagen), because design is a national passion and a point of pride. People are very careful to have incredibly well crafted things in their home."

Kristi has also taken the time to forge friendships with unlikely people within the industry. Before the weekend workshop was over, she was able to connect with a design student at the University of Oregon and visit her to see her portfolio of work.

She also remains close to a woman she met in her first design class. As she describes it, "She has this insanely powerful job (at a high profile athletic apparel company) and a small child, but (our mutual interest in design) keeps us in contact."

### Kristi's Advice

"Trust the information your spirit…is giving you and if something isn't working…take some kind of action. Taking action leads to something.

And the other thing is—and I'm still guilty of this—let go of wanting to know the end goal when you start the journey—sometimes you just need to start. Giving yourself the leeway to start before you know helps."

\*\*\*

**Want to hear more of Kristi's Story?  Listen to the audio of Kristi describing her career journey at**

**www.Start2Bloom.com**

\*\*\*

# CHAPTER 8

*Breaking Ground*

**Step #3: Get Connected to the Right People**

"When we ask for advice,

we are usually looking for an accomplice."

-- Marquis de la Grange

Raise your hand if you ever got a job because you previously knew the person who hired you.

You too, huh?

When I ask this in my classes, most of the hands go up immediately… and then when I mention babysitting or lawn mowing, the rest of the hands go up.

Even in our high-tech world of enormous websites listing thousands and thousands of jobs, there's just no substitute for knowing the right people at the right time. These are the folks who know you, know your work, and have fallen in love with you a little bit. They become your champions… the people who somehow manage to bring you onboard even in the middle of the coldest and darkest of hiring freezes. (Yes, it really does happen.)

Right now, you might be sitting there nodding your head in agreement—and then this thought will jump to mind, "But I must not know the right people, or I'd already have a new job!"

Therein lies the challenge. How do you meet the right people—your future accomplices—who not only cheer when you cross the finish line with a great new career, but also are the reason you're in the race in the first place?

When I ask this question in class, inevitably a student will bring up the dreaded "N" word...Networking. (Gasp!)

Does the mere mention of the word "networking" strike terror in your heart?

Do you conjure up images of watery cocktails, dry hors d'oeurves, and either uncomfortable small talk or boring business chat?

Does it make you want to plug your ears and sing, "La,la,la,la,la?"

If so, you're not the only one. To be honest, I'm not a big fan of most of the activities that are associated with traditional business networking. I haven't done much of it in my career, and I heartily encourage you to abandon this activity and trade up to a much more exciting and sustainable approach.

Even if you're the kind of person who loves meeting new people and chatting up a room, you might be more worried about being liked than anything else. This means that all that interacting really isn't adding up to anything that will blossom.

No matter whether you're a wallflower or life of the party, there's definitely a better way to make the most of meeting new people.

It all begins with understanding the concept of "your people."

*"Your People"*

Is everyone you meet your cup of tea?

Of course not! There are people you instantly like, people you're mildly interested in, and people you don't care for.

"Your people" are the ones you resonate with. There's often a meeting of the minds, shared values, similar interests, and a natural flow to the conversation. In short, they are the people that you connect with even though you're not trying very hard.

Hallelujah!

These are the people you're looking for in this big social career experiment.

"Your people" are the ones who will take an avid interest in what you're up to. They'll pick you up when you're feeling knocked down. They'll search their mental Rolodex when you need a resource. They have the attitude that you can and will succeed at whatever you're aiming to accomplish.

I'm betting the next question you'd like to ask me is, "Where do I find my people?"

It's not as hard as you think…

**The Ultimate Treasure Hunt**

Don't you just love *Antiques Roadshow*?

Just in case you've never heard of it—let me fill you in.

Found on PBS, this is a TV show that captures the excitement of a group of experts who travel around the country providing appraisals of antiques and collectibles. Everyday folks show up at their local convention center toting family heirlooms, dusty attic wares, and garage sale finds.

It's big fun to witness people like you and me discovering the value of things they've often been either ignoring or overlooking for years.

Believe it or not, you have the equivalent of Antiques Roadshow in your very own "attic." But I'm not talking about stuff; no, I'm talking about people.

### *Your "Inner Circle"*

Your "Inner Circle" is filled with the people that you know best. That's right: your family, your neighbors, your friends, and your co-workers can often turn out to be your very own treasure chest of ideas, information, and connections.

I think this is the best of news, since it's generally much easier to talk to people you already know than to walk up to a complete stranger and strike up a conversation.

Granted, not everyone in your inner circle will "get" what you're trying to do. They may not provide the ideas or encouragement you're looking for. That's OK—it just means they aren't the one to point you in the right direction. It's a sign to move on to someone else. It's all a part of the exploration process to find "your people."

### *"Your Step-People"*

No, "your step-people" are not folks who've married their way into your life!

Instead, these are the people who are one step removed from your innermost circle of acquaintances. These are the friends of friends, the co-workers of former co-workers, and the links of your links on LinkedIn.

In the process that's described in the rest of this book, you can expect that some of your step-people will move up to become "your people." And eventually some of those will move into your inner circle as colleagues.

### Your "Bacon Number"

Have you heard of the Kevin Bacon Game?

According to Wikipedia:

"The Kevin Bacon game is a trivia game based on the concept of the small world phenomenon and rests on the assumption that any individual can be linked through his or her film roles to actor Kevin Bacon within six steps. The name of the game is a play on the 'six degrees of separation' concept. The game requires a group of players to try to connect any individual to Kevin Bacon as quickly as possible and in as few links as possible."

Thus, a "Bacon Number" is the number of links an actor has to Kevin Bacon.

Unless you're an actor, this might not be making much sense. So let me explain how this really is relevant to you.

The definition of the Kevin Bacon Game includes a reference to the small world phenomenon, or six degrees of separation. Again, deferring to Wikipedia brings us to this definition:

"Six degrees of separation refers to the idea that everyone is on average approximately six steps away, by way of introduction, from any other person on Earth, so that a chain of, "a friend of a friend" statements can be made, on average, to connect any two people in six steps or fewer."

Imagine that! You could be less than six acquaintances away from knowing the right person to hire you into your perfect work. It's a small world after all! You just have to be willing to connect the dots...

**Connecting the Dots**

Are you ready to learn the process for getting to your ultimate accomplice? (By that I mean the person who is going to hire you to do your perfect work.) I hope so, because ready or not—here we go!

*Start with Reflection*

You did a lot of hard work in Steps 1 and 2 of the Plant Yourself Where You Will Bloom process. You've taken the time to really discover who you are and what you want. You've also explored the new world of work and the bouquet of opportunities it offers.

Reflecting on all that you've discovered, what stands out for you?

Are you most excited about using your greatest talents? Or is it more about exploring a truly compelling interest? Maybe expressing your values wants to take center stage.

Whichever it is, one thing is probably sure: you have questions that you'd like to get answered.

To begin with, make a list of the questions that you have regarding the thing (or things) standing out for you.

For example, maybe you want to know:

- All the different ways you could be using your talent.
- What's going on in a particular industry—from an insider's perspective
- The latest efforts to support a particular cause
- How a fading industry is trying to revive itself
- The next product a particular company is planning to release

### *Make a list of your inner circle*

It's time to make a list of everyone you know really well. You might even want to make a list of people that you sort of know, too. Everyone in your family, your neighbors, your friends, current and former coworkers, fellow hobbyists, the parents of your kids' friends, members of your church, your mailman, hairdresser, banker, mechanic, bartender…you get the drift. Anyone that you come into contact with and know on a first name basis is fair game.

This is the point where you might be getting a glimpse of the true value of the social media platforms like Facebook, LinkedIn, and Twitter (not to mention Pinterest, Google+, and many others.) Many of those in your inner circle are active on one or more of these sites—which means your inner circle list already exists!

And don't overlook the goldmine in your email address book…all those people are just a few clicks away.

### *Cross-match*

Now you can look at the questions you want answered (based on your reflection) and see who in your inner circle might be able to answer your question, or might know someone who can answer it.

If you feel you don't know who in your inner circle might be able to answer your question, then you'll just have to start working through the list.

Here's an important caveat: Start with the person who is most on your side. This is the person who really has your best interest at heart. Try not to pick someone who has a lot invested in the direction you ultimately choose. Sometimes they're just too worried about you (and themselves) to be objective and supportive.

My student Jeff is a great example of getting great results from starting close to home to find out who might be able to answer his questions.

Jeff was curious about a company in his town that was in a completely different field than his current employer. Although he didn't feel he had a particularly great story to tell in terms of industry experience, he remembered that he had a friend who worked there. He picked up the phone and asked her for some advice about the company.

Jeff's friend put him in touch with another manager in her company, and they met for an advice chat. A few months later, the manager called saying that she had a job opening—one that hadn't even been posted yet. Long story short, he got the job!

### *Pick a time to talk*

It's up to you whether you want to be casual or formal about asking your questions. Sometimes just striking up a casual conversation with someone you know is all you need to get the ball rolling. But if you feel you'd like a person to be a bit more prepared, you might consider taking a more formal approach.

## Advice Chat

This more formal approach, conducting an advice chat, is one I learned from the very first career book I ever read: Nancy Anderson's *Work with Passion.*

An advice chat is the opportunity to sit down with someone and literally ask for their advice in an area of their expertise.

This is different from an informational interview. Very different. As in…please read this section very carefully!

### *Just Say No to Informational Interviews*

The last thing you want to do in this process is to ask someone for an informational interview.

Why?

Because the word interview is automatically linked with the concept of a *job*.

In a challenging economic environment, jobs seem hard to come by. If a person's organization claims it isn't hiring, that person will not want to be in the uncomfortable position of telling you they can't hire you. They'll simply tell you they don't have time to talk to you. And this usually isn't the case.

Instead, if you ask to talk to them for a few minutes and get their advice about some questions you have, they are far more likely to respond favorably.

Why?

Because everyone loves to give advice!

It's flattering to be asked your opinion. Most people see giving advice as being helpful. And most people desperately want to be helpful whenever they can.


### *Scheduling an Advice Chat*

It's easiest to set up an advice chat with someone that you already know. You can simply ask them for twenty or thirty minutes of their time to ask some questions and get their advice. Since they know you, they're likely to say yes.

If the person you want to connect with is not in your inner circle—let's say they're one of your step-people—you will want your mutual acquaintance to introduce you somehow. This is known as a "warm introduction." Email is an easy choice for getting this accomplished. Just have your inner circle member send an email introducing you and letting them know you have some questions and need their advice.

Now you have permission to reach out to that contact directly. They're expecting to hear from you and will feel far less threatened than if you were to send them an email directly. (This is called a "cold call" and usually makes everyone involved feel uncomfortable.)

### *Preparing for the Advice Chat*

Once you have your advice chat scheduled, it's time to compile your list of questions. If you can do enough research to really understand who your contact is, it will make it far easier to know what kinds of things to ask them.

In general, there are three areas from which to draw questions: their personal situation, which means their particular job and career path, the company they work for, and their industry.

### *Conducting the Advice Chat*

This is the fun part!

Really, anything goes in this conversation because it's more of a chat than anything else. Whatever you do, don't treat it like an interview! This is your opportunity to really get to know this person and get some valuable advice about how to move forward in your exploration. It's far closer to creating a friendship than it is to anything remotely related to job hunting.

Let me share a few tips to help make sure this is a successful encounter:

Be curious. Curiosity is one of the most attractive places a person can come from. When you're curious, you're open to possibilities and are far more likely to see connections between unexpected things.

Listen. Remember the old adage that you have two ears and one mouth and it's wisest to use them in the same proportion. Picture yourself being a sponge—soaking up as many ideas as you possibly can.

Take lots of notes. When you're hanging on every word it shows that you're very respectful of the other person's expertise.

Mind the clock. If you've asked for 20 or 30 minutes, acknowledge when you've reached that time. They may be willing to spend more time with you, which is great.

Bring your questions. It's perfectly fine to bring in the questions you've prepared. But be willing to abandon your pre-work if you find the conversation is naturally going in a far more interesting direction.

These final two tips are probably the most important of all:

*Be sure to ask who else they think can give you some advice.*

This is the only way you can keep the ball rolling in this process. Without another person to speak with, you reach a dead end and could easily become discouraged.

And finally:

*Never, ever, ever put a resume in front of someone in an advice chat.*

Resumes are always associated with job seeking. At this stage of the game, you are not ready to look for a job. You're still too busy putting together all of the pieces of the puzzle in the pursuit of your perfect work. If someone asks you for a resume, say that because you haven't been actively job-hunting, you don't have one. Let them know you're really just looking for advice right now.

Remember—anything you do that seems related to the traditional job search runs the risk of making your contact shut down. And what you really want is for his or her mind and heart to be wide open and receptive to who you're becoming—not what a white piece of paper with black squiggles says about your past.

Years ago, when my husband and I decided to move our family from California to Portland, Oregon, we began the process of job hunting.

I asked a current co-worker if she knew anyone in Portland that I could talk to. She put me in touch with the president of a small company in my industry. I contacted him to set up an advice chat using her name as a reference, and he immediately said yes.

We had one meeting, and he offered me a job in his company. He never even asked me for a resume!

### *Following up after the Advice Chat*

Without fail, you must send a thank you note following every advice chat. You can keep it very simple by thanking them for their time and mentioning one or two things that you learned from them in the conversation. Let them know you'll be following up with the person they referred you to (hopefully you remembered to ask them to give you a warm introduction!) and that you'll keep them posted on your progress.

*****************

Now you understand the non-networking way of discovering and developing relationships with the right people. And you can see the sheer beauty of the advice chat approach. Move on to the next chapter to discover the very best way to keep all your new accomplices invested and engaged in your career success.

# *Jeff's Story*
## Meet the Right People
## and Make it a Point to Stay In Touch

What do you do when you're tired, frustrated and overworked—but you haven't quite put your finger on what's actually making you unhappy in your work? You know you need to make a change, but how will you figure it out and avoid going down the wrong road yet again?

Meet Jeff. Smart, honest, and adventurous. When he came to my series of career classes, he felt he was at a crossroads and needed to answer an important question for himself—one that he wants to pass along to you to answer as well…

"Do you dislike your career or do you dislike the place you're doing it? Sometimes it's hard to separate the two."

But separate the two is exactly what he was finally able to do. Jeff realized that life/work balance was not a priority in his current company, and that it was important enough to him to make it a requirement of his next employer.

The only question left was how to find the local companies that shared his values.

### Jeff's Path to a New Job

Luckily, Jeff's the kind of guy who knows how to take expert advice. He believed what he learned in my class…that the easiest place to start, when it comes to getting connected to the right people, is usually with the people you already know.

With that bit of clarity, he decided to chat it up with friends to find the kind of company that would honor his value of life/work balance.

"Yes, it's true. It's all about who you know. It all started with a friend, just asking her how she liked working at (her company). Then, by chance, she knew of a job opening in a few months. I was able to get an (advice chat) with the hiring manager months before the job posted. It was a low-pressure way to find out more about the position and company. After that, I made it a point to stay in touch with her. When it came time for the job to be posted, she personally e-mailed me to let me know it was there. The second interview was great, being that I already knew her a little bit!"

Because he took the time to stay in touch with his new contact, she automatically thought of him when the job came open. If he hadn't stayed connected, well…out of sight is out of mind, right?

Jeff also discovered that the best interviews are the ones with the least pressure. At the time of his first advice chat, there was no job opening. This meant the meeting was more of a friendly chat with a colleague. Because of this, Jeff was able to ask important questions in a non-threatening way.

### Jeff's Career Epiphany

Throughout his search, Jeff stayed committed to understanding what needed to change for him to be happy. As it turned out, his unhappiness wasn't about his day-to-day responsibilities, it was about whether the company created a healthy work environment for employees.

"Even if I someday get tired of my position, I know that this (new) company fits my values and lifestyle. And maybe that's the biggest win from this whole process."

**Jeff's Advice**

"Interview question books are outdated. In my opinion, it's far more important to think about the thought process—the way you work daily—and not so much about memorizing 100 potential interview questions.

(Instead, ask yourself) what are your motivations? Why did you complete that project the way you did? Why are you that type of a manager? Maybe my interviews were (non-traditional), but there weren't many standard questions that these books/websites make you think there will be. It's more important just to know yourself."

***

**Want to hear more inspiring stories?**

**Listen to the audios of my clients describing their career journeys at www.Start2Bloom.com**

***

# CHAPTER 9

*Tilling the Soil*

**Step #4: Create and Build Your Community**

"Relationships of trust depend on our willingness

to look not only to our own interests,

but also the interests of others."

--Peter Farquharson

Once you're meeting the right people, you can't just leave them parked out by the curb. You have to invite them in once in a while for cake and coffee and a little gossip!

Keep in mind that some relationships take time to bloom. Upon a first meeting, you may not recognize how you can support each other immediately. But the time could definitely come when you have more to offer. The opportunity will be lost if you don't stay in touch, though.

It's important to maintain your accomplices as lifetime connections. You'll want to cultivate these relationships through careful nurturing.

Rest assured—I'm not talking about creating an artificial, contrived way to stay in touch (that's almost as impersonal as traditional networking!)

I'm talking about developing an exciting reason to share information and discoveries. I'm talking about linking together your "tribe" of industry peeps in a way that stimulates their creativity and challenges them to continue growing in the field, too.

Before I go too much further, though, I have a question for you:

Just how excited are you about this new career you're embarking upon?

Excited enough to create a pet project around which you can rally all your like-passioned contacts? I have to say, this is the litmus test. This is what separates the women from the girls when it comes to demonstrating just how meaningful your new career is to you.

Here's why…

### Making "A" Difference vs. Making "The" Difference

I meet with a lot of people who are struggling with their careers. When I ask them what's not working for them, the one thing I hear more often than not is, "I just want to make a difference!"

I do think most people are really sincere when they say this, but I have to wonder if it's actually the truth! Because *everything* you do makes a difference. If you drop a pebble in a puddle, you will see ripples—you're making a difference in that puddle. But there's an important distinction between making "A" difference and making "THE" difference you want to make.

For example, let's say you're a talented baker who loves serving people chocolate treats. If you bake a batch of brownies and take them into the office, thereby knocking three co-workers off their diets—instead of appreciating you, they might end up resenting you! That's making "A" difference.

If, however, you bake a batch of brownies that you then sell in your very own bakery—and everyone who walks through the door is there because your delicious brownies make them happy—then you've made "the" difference you want to make.

Where would our world be if Ghandi, Mother Theresa, or Martin Luther King, Jr. hadn't made "THE" difference they set out to make?

And where will the world be if you don't?

When you are making "the" difference you want to be making, your career is far more meaningful to you.

## Choosing a Project

When you care deeply about something, you're willing to devote all kinds of time to it. So it makes sense that your pet project will be a reflection of your greatest talents, interests, and knowledge.

In choosing a pet project, the key questions to ask yourself are: what fascinates you about this new field; what do you know something about; what would you like to spend time learning about; and, what are you already good at?

If you've done the work of Step 1 to plant yourself where you will bloom, you will have answers to these questions. And it's possible that your project will naturally leap to your mind. But in case it doesn't, here are a few examples of possible projects:

- Create a blog
- Develop a 100-day challenge
- Establish a scholarship
- Hold a fundraiser
- Write a book
- Plan an event
- Develop an app
- Start up a company

- Start a small non-profit
- Teach a community college class
- Develop a website
- Plan a speaking tour
- Design a class for kids
- Create a movement
- Open a store on Etsy
- Create a digital game

My client DeeDee's core value is creativity. Most days she can be found working on one creative project or another. She is an award-winning costume designer, a children's book author, a terrific cook, and quite an accomplished crafter.

A few years ago, DeeDee trained to become a Creativity Coach. To make the transition into this work, and to become a recognized leader in the field, she created a blog as her pet project. She based it on the change she most wished to create in the world: abolishing negativity. As a result, she is now in year four of "The Campaign for Creativity to Banish Negativity." (Here's the link: http://www.createtofeelgreat.blogspot.com/)

DeeDee set a goal to complete one creative project a week, and to blog about her creative experience. She shares her insights (and details about her craft projects) with an ever-growing, international following.

DeeDee's story provides a great example of how you can combine various talents, interests, and values to create a project that speaks to your heart and connects you to your people.

### *Giving Your Project a Home*

As with any pet, your project will need a "home."

The great news is that never before has it been so easy to create a virtual "home" where your project can live and grow. I am, of course, referring to the online world—which probably began as someone's pet project! The concept here is that you are developing a place for your accomplices to meet, support, share, and stay connected to your project. The bonus is that they are also staying connected to you—which means you are front and center in their minds. Which is important when the time comes for them to hire someone fantastic!

One of the easiest virtual homes is a blog or a social networking site. Think Facebook and LinkedIn. (Even Twitter is a viable option as a home for a pet project. That's what hashtags are all about.)

On Facebook, you can either establish a business page or start a group. And your accomplices don't even have to join Facebook in order to participate.

To learn more about creating a virtual home for your project, I recommend the "…for Dummies" series of books about these online sites, or doing some old-fashioned online research.

### *Rally the Accomplices*

Once you've chosen a project and have an appropriate home, it's time to invite your contacts to become involved. One of the best times to do this is as you're doing your advice chats. But even if you establish your pet project after you've met someone, you can still create a launch of the project and invite all the contacts in your inner circle.

Don't be intimidated by the term "launch." A launch is simply an announcement that you've created your project and an invitation for people to become a part of it. Simplicity is the name of the game here.

Keep in mind that a key part of developing this community of accomplices is to find a way to keep them involved. Remember how happy people are to give you advice? Be sure to ask them regularly what they think about how you're moving forward. Ask them to submit comments on your blog, or post articles in your group.

*****************

One of the invaluable side benefits in this process is the fact that you are also linking your contacts to one another—you are building a community in your new industry.

This is what's known as a value-add, and it's a way of "paying back" the people who have been so kindly giving you their advice. You are linking them together in a way that benefits everyone participating.

And there's one more priceless benefit—you will be seen as a leader in your new field. When you take this sort of initiative, people are impressed. Inevitably, you'll be brought to the attention of the movers and shakers of your industry, and these are the kind of people who like to keep their alliances strong. You will find mentors and partners and, yes…dare I say it? Potentially some really terrific bosses!

## DeeDee's Story
### The Box of Chocolate
### Being Shared Around the Room

What do you do when you're in a toxic work environment and know you need to get out, but you have so many different things you'd like to express about yourself that it seems impossible to choose just one career?

Meet DeeDee. Creative, compassionate, and owner of a great big personal vision. When DeeDee hired me as her career coach, she was absolutely miserable in her 9–5 job doing front office work for a local retailer. She had an unshakeable feeling that her life was destined to be bigger than she was living it—that she was meant to be contributing more.

In our very first session, she knew that her creative spirit needed to fly far and wide. "Freedom" became her new buzzword, and she immediately set to figuring out how to incorporate it into all aspects of her life.

### DeeDee's Career Epiphany

Creativity and self-expression are qualities that DeeDee had seen in herself since childhood. "I remember just spending hours and hours drawing and writing as a kid. You know this is something we lock away sometimes… for whatever reason…we got busy or something. "

A huge part of DeeDee's epiphany was recognizing those artistic parts of herself that had been tucked away and acknowledging that they needed to come out. Later she realized that an important aspect of her professional pursuits would include setting free the inner artists of other people, as well.

As she puts it, "I think we all have gifts; [our job is] finding and unwrapping them. It is the box of chocolate being shared around the room."

## DeeDee's Journey to a New Career

In addition to being outstandingly creative, DeeDee is also a very logical woman. She knew that creativity and self-expression needed to be major aspects of her day-to-day life, but she also knew that the bills needed to be paid.

With some help from her husband, she strategized a way to work at a fulfilling part-time office job with a boss she adored, thus freeing up time to launch artistic projects that would also generate some income. She revived her former career in costume design, but vowed only to take on projects that made her heart happy. And she also started a small venture making custom hats that she sold in boutiques around town.

Over the years, DeeDee's profit centers (the different ways she makes money using her creative talents) have shifted and evolved. Always consistent, though, is her commitment to doing the things that she enjoys the most.

## DeeDee's Big Vision

Several years ago, DeeDee gave herself a huge challenge. She had been intrigued by the story of *Julie and Julia*—the tale of how an unknown blogger gained worldwide recognition by writing about her journey to achieving a major goal, that of cooking all of the recipes in Julia Child's *Mastering the Art of French Cooking*.

Since DeeDee's inner Jane Austen was also beginning to surface, writing a blog as a pet project was a logical choice. DeeDee realized that the difference she wanted to make in the world was ridding it of negativity through creativity.

The purpose of DeeDee's blog was to connect with other inspired innovators in the online community and encourage them to engage in creative projects on a weekly basis. As DeeDee completes her weekly craft project, she gives instructions and reflects on the lessons she's learning through being creative. The result? She's feeding her need for self expression, making global connections, furthering her vision of banishing negativity in the world, and accomplishing fun projects every week.

The blog has been successful beyond her initial expectations, and she now has contacts around the world to share and support her artistic dreams.

She says, "The personal fulfillment is a wonderfully gratifying feeling, but the sense of community is humbling."

\*\*\*

**Want to hear more of DeeDee's Story?  Listen to the audio of DeeDee describing her career journey at**

**www.Start2Bloom.com**

\*\*\*

# CHAPTER 10

*Adding Food, Water, and Sunshine*

**Step #5: Decide How to Make Money**

"It isn't about money, fame or power. It's about will, dedication, commitment and knowing your self-worth. You can be poor as dirt and have those traits. Money can't buy you values. You just need to know what is important to you and then feel secure in your pursuit to achieve that."

-- Jennifer Hudson

How much money do you want to make?

Seems like a fairly straightforward question, but you might be surprised to discover that you don't really know the answer.

If you think you just want enough money to be able to pay the bills, I will challenge you to think bigger than that. It's a great, big, exciting world out there. So much to see and do! Don't sell yourself short on having enough money to live the life you really want to be living.

So why am I bringing this up?

Perhaps it starts with the fact that most people don't really know how much money they actually need. Many of us tend to live our lives with a vague idea of how much we're spending, how much we need to be saving, what should be in an emergency account, etc. Knowing this information is an important step in becoming financially independent.

**Financial Independence**

Although financial independence is a goal for just about everyone, do we really know what it means to be financially independent? If we're using Bill Gates or Warren Buffet or Oprah Winfrey as a measure, no wonder most of us feel pretty hopeless. As a result, expectations for income get lower and lower although the desire for more money stays firmly in place.

So let's start with taking a run at defining financial independence, and then we'll get into the nitty gritty of your preferences for how much money you need and want to be making in your perfect work.

*Defining Financial Independence*

Here's a running start to the task of defining Financial Independence:

• Being able to live indefinitely without having to work

• When the revenue generated by your assets exceeds your expenses. (It doesn't matter how much money your assets generate as long as it exceeds your expenses…could be $100 or $1,000,000)

  • A feeling or an attitude marked by a lack of fear about money

  • Coming from a place of abundance rather than lack

Before we go too much further, there's something I just have to mention. Because it might trip you up on your path to perfect work.

### Confusion about Money is the Real Dreamkiller

Barbara Sher, career author, says isolation is the real dreamkiller. I disagree; I think the culprit is actually confusion about money. I think that most people would happily leap to doing their perfect work if they weren't scared to death that they wouldn't be able to make enough money to initially cover their bills and ultimately be financially independent.

Let's take this opportunity to clear up as much confusion as we can— so that you can confidently claim your preferences around money and get further clarity regarding your perfect work.

#### *Do What You Love and the Money Will Follow*

Back in the '80s, Marsha Sinetar wrote a very popular book with this title. Although it stirred up strong emotions at the time, nowadays I think the message has been misconstrued.

Most people think this implies that they will make all the money they want once they launch into their perfect work. At the same time, most people are suspicious that this is too good to be true.

If only it really *were* that easy!

#### *If You Build It, They Will Come*

Remember this phrase: "You have to be willing to learn and then take the right actions."

This is an important one to take to heart. Unlike Kevin Costner's character in the movie, "Field of Dreams," the rest of us have to take an extra step:

If You Build It and *Tell Them About It,* They Will Come.

This means you have to be willing to shout it out to the world. Some people call this selling or marketing. Either way, the bottom line this time is that you again have to make connections with the right people—the people who need your goods or services—and you have to give them the opportunity to buy from you.

This holds true whether you are an entrepreneur or are looking for an employer. You can't be a best-kept secret and expect to achieve financial success.

### *Money = Success*

How do you define success in your career?

If you're like most people, the first thing that pops to mind is a number…your income, to be exact.

Truth is, defining success solely by income is a very limiting definition.

Yes, money is important—for reasons we'll discuss in the next section. But there are other aspects of success that are equally (dare I say more?) important. For example: satisfaction and reward; personal growth; accomplishment; making the difference you want to be making.

Take the time to expand your definition of success to include more than just your income. This will put money back into perspective, where it belongs.

### *I Can't Be Financially Irresponsible*

I have yet to meet a single soul who didn't have some level of need for economic security.

It's a fact that our society is based on a monetary system. It's difficult (although not impossible) to live without exchanging money for goods and services.

So yes, it's important to be financially responsible. And the good news is that making the leap to your perfect work never requires financial irresponsibility. You may need a really great transition strategy, though.

When I found career coaching as my calling, I put together an 18-month transition plan that had me working in my current full-time job and saving as much as $20,000 as a financial cushion for my business. I was simply unwilling to jeopardize my home and my family's well-being. As a result, I ended up making the leap sooner (because my company closed its doors after six months) but I had the money that I needed to make it all work.

Over the years, I have consistently strategized the best ways to achieve my financial goals. The bottom line is: you never have to compromise your financial needs in order to make the leap to your perfect work. You just have to be willing to keep a clear financial plan and make the smartest choices.

**Financial Wizard 101**

Let's talk a little about how you can discover your own financial preferences. It may sound odd to think that you have a unique set of preferences around money. After all, everyone wants to be rich, right?

Actually, no! I've met plenty of people who are content to achieve financial independence without defining it as being "rich." I've heard people define their preference as financial serenity, financial security, and financial peace of mind, to name just a few.

Whatever you prefer, it's important to get it out on the table, so that you have the best shot at making your financial dreams a reality.

*Life in the Fast Lane*

Although there are people who want to make a lot of money just for the sake of making a lot of money, for most of us, it's about having options.

And most of those options relate to our desired lifestyle.

Whether you've taken the time to articulate it or not, you have a vision of the kind of lifestyle you would like to be living. This includes where you live, how you dress, what you drive, your recreational activities, travel, etc.

When you capture your lifestyle vision, you can get a more accurate gauge of how much money you'd prefer to be making.


*Money Set-Points*

Financial gurus tell us that just as it's probable that we have set-points for our weight, we also have them for our cash flow. Basically, this means that you are "accustomed" to managing a certain amount of money—you're comfortable with a certain level of cash coming in and going out.

You actually have specific systems in place that manage your money. This includes checking and savings accounts as well as investments, bills and other expenses, etc. Unless you do something to change your systems that in turn influences a change of that money set-point, you're unlikely to break through to another level.

This theory explains why people who hit the big lottery jackpots are often broke within just a few years. Their systems—both internal and external—simply can't handle the new rush of energy in the form of cash. So they have to get rid of it as soon as possible so that they can return to that comfortable cash set-point.

Can you see what your money set-point is? If you average your income over the last several years, you'll come close to pinpointing it. What would it take for you to change your set-point? What systems could you create now that would allow for an increase (or even a decrease) with which you can be comfortable?

### *Abundance vs. Lack*

Do you see the world as a place of abundance? Does all the beauty, or the variety of people, or even just the breakfast options on Denny's menu ever overwhelm you?

It's possible to either see the world as an abundant place or one of lack. And nothing illustrates this point better than money.

Take some time to decide whether you believe you can have all the money you want, or whether the world is limiting you somehow. The answer might surprise you—and upping your abundance mentality can change everything.

Here's a fun exercise that I share with my clients: for one week, keep a running list of everything that indicates just how much money there is in the world. You might notice all the cash that changes hands in a fast-food restaurant. You might notice a surprise check in your mailbox one day. You might add up your income over all the years you've been working. You might add up all the money you could save if you used all the coupons in your Sunday paper. The possibilities are enormous…you might even say abundant!

The idea is to have fun and to begin to see just how much financial abundance there really is in this great big world of ours.

### *Show Me the Money*

Yes, I think Jerry Maguire is one of the greatest "perfect work" movies ever made. In the film, "Show me the money" becomes the mantra for both Jerry and his only client, Rod Tidwell. In the end, we learn that money is

just one reward that comes from putting your heart and soul into everything you do.

Have you ever wondered where that money comes from, though?

Years ago I read about a spiritual leader whose followers wanted to
build a new temple for worship. The leader announced the plans, but his
financial leaders were aghast since they didn't have the cash to pay for the
building. They asked him where he expected the money to come from
and his reply was, "From wherever it is now." Eventually, they did attract
the money from wherever it was, and they were able to build their temple.

Can this be true in our lives, as well? That when we are following are
hearts and pouring ourselves into making a dream come true, we can bring
the money to us no matter where it is right now?

Hmmmmm..........

### Choosing the Right Business Model

Once you've decided to be completely honest about your financial situation as well as your future hopes and dreams, you can begin to choose the
right business model to make the kind of money you want to be making.

And yes…no matter what your perfect work is, you can make the kind
of money you hope to be making…even if you're a fledgling artist with
your eyes on making millions.

Because the truth is that in any industry, there are people who make a
ton of money and people who make no money at all—and everyone else
falls somewhere in the middle.

### *Learning from Suze Orman*

Let's look at Suze Orman as an example of choosing the right business model for the money you want to be making.

For decades, Suze has had a career in the financial world.

She started out as a stockbroker working in a brokerage house. This particular business model (being an employee in this kind of an organization) pays a certain amount of money. Not much, by the way.

Eventually, Suze moved into the world of personal finance as a financial planner. This business model (sometimes an employee of an organization; sometimes working independently but representing certain investment products) pays a different amount of money.

Finally, Suze moved into the world of personal finance as an information provider. She writes books and travels the country speaking and doing seminars. She has appeared on countless talk shows, and even has her own. This business model pays on a very different scale—some people make quite a bit of money, while others struggle to gain the level of fame of a Suze Orman. (By the way, if this is your perfect work and you want to be a multi-millionaire, you might want to use Suze's business model!)

So, Suze was always in the same industry of personal finance (which arose from her fascination with money), but at different points she used very different business models, leading to very different income levels.

Only one thing dictates how much money you can make in any given industry: which business model you choose to follow.

The bottom line is that you have to know *how* to make money in order to make money. And the best short-cut to learning how it's done in any given industry is to identify the people who are making the kind of money you want, learn from them, and follow the same business model.

This might look like establishing a formal personal mentorship, or it might look like learning from them from a distance. Either way, you have to be willing to learn and then take the right actions to find financial success in any field or industry.

### *Work with Your Life*

Earlier in this book, we talked about the importance of loving your work, working with love, and working with your life.

At this stage of the game, it's important to reflect on all three of these areas to be sure that the business model you're choosing will honor the truth of who you are.

Earlier I mentioned that your perfect work never requires you to be financially irresponsible. Actually, it never requires you to be irresponsible about *any* aspect of your life.

While you are exploring business models, if any element of a model makes you feel like you have to compromise in some way, it's a good idea to keep searching for another model. When you hit on the right one, you'll know it.

### *Sticking With It*

I'd be remiss if I led you to believe that to make the money you want all you need to do is discover your perfect work and find the right business model.

Maybe the biggest challenge of all is to stick with it long enough to see the success you're looking for.

Thomas Edison said, "Many of life's failures are people who did not realize how close they were to success when they gave up."

Don't give up.

*****************

Whether your goal is financial independence, security, serenity, or simply peace of mind…it's achievable with three important elements:

Knowing what you want in terms of money; finding the right business model to attain your objectives; and sticking with it until it happens.

Please, please, please…don't let money be your dreamkiller!

## *Tom's Story*
### Stay Focused and Be Smart
### About Growing a Prosperous Business

What do you do when you've experienced a major life change and the old way of doing your work simply isn't going to fit well with your new lifestyle? And what do you do if you're not entirely ready to throw out the baby with the bathwater—as in, change your career completely?

Meet Tom. Kind, cogent, and Dad of the Year. When he came to my series of career classes, he was a new parent and his interests had shifted away from managing a hectic work schedule to finding more time for family and fun. His job as the manager of a travel agency left him unfulfilled and overworked. He had an inkling that there had to be better opportunities out there.

### Tom's Path to a New Way of Making Money Using His Strengths

While attending my class, Tom discovered that he wasn't the only one at a crossroads. Connecting with other people who wanted to change their professional circumstances was a huge motivator for Tom.

"Regardless of the circumstances you're in, whether you're in a challenging position or your work situation has suddenly changed or whatever, I think that a constructive and supportive social environment is really key," he said.

Having the support and feedback of different people opened up Tom to perspectives he had never considered before. One thing I constantly hear is that my students begin to think differently and, consequently, are open to new opportunities and possibilities they never dreamed of. For Tom, it was getting out of his comfort zone through classes, retreats, volunteering, and trying out social and professional groups like Toastmasters.

### Tom's Career Epiphany

Tom's "aha!" came when he realized that he wanted his job to involve fostering connections with other people, and so having a strong network was crucial to his success.

Tom decided to branch out on his own professionally after receiving many calls from former customers who sought out his services. He knew he wanted to be his own boss and not be a "slave to a storefront," as he puts it, so he figured out how to run his own travel business with the help of a client who offered up his extra office space.

### Where is Tom Now?

After a few months, Tom sat back and looked at all he had accomplished after taking a few small steps out of his comfort zone.

"What did strike me was that I could control the amount of time that I was working so I could have more of myself to give to my family, to my daughter, and to my life at home. I wasn't feeling like I needed to work 12 hours a day or 80 hours a week, like I had been doing for so many years."

After reevaluating his needs and wants, Tom decided that spending time with his family was the most important aspect to managing his time and career, but not the only goal on his horizon. "I was entirely convinced that I could actually make a living of some sort, and contribute to the household financially.

I not only proved to myself that I could do that but that I could be smart about growing a prosperous business as long as I stayed focused."

### Tom's Advice

Tom's strategy boils down to the basics: "If there was ever an epiphany along the way, [it] was being able to understand that staying focused on what you know how to do and what you do really well feeds the other stuff."

\*\*\*

**Want to hear more of Tom's story? Listen to the audio of Tom describing his career journey at**

**www.Start2Bloom.com**

\*\*\*

# CHAPTER 11

## *Planting the Seedling*

**Step #6: Strategize Your Transition**

"The most dangerous strategy

is to jump a chasm in two leaps."

-- Benjamin Disraeli

Whew! We've come a long way.

Now you're thoroughly schooled on the importance of five key things: discovering yourself; discovering the new world of work; meeting the right people; creating a pet project to build your community; and finding the right business model that meets your unique needs.

You're ready to make the leap now, right? Just give up the day job and plunge head first into your perfect work…

What? You're not so sure about that?

Good! But don't give up on me now. We're ready to get practical and rational about how you will make the leap to your perfect work. It's all about creating the perfect strategy for your particular situation.

Before we actually start to strategize, let's make sure we're on the same page as to what it means to strategize and how to go about doing it.

**Defining Strategy**

What are some characteristics of a strategy?

- A strategy is how you will get from where you are to where you want to be

- A strategy is the "how," the destination is the "what"

- There can be several different possible strategies for reaching any destination

- Your best strategy is based on your own personal strengths and experience

- Strategies are practical, rational, and logical

- A strategy is usually broken down into smaller stages and then steps within each stage

Now that you have a basic understanding of what a strategy is, you also need to get clear on what it means to strategize.

**The Process of Strategizing**

It's usually helpful to have a step-by-step description of a process. Here are the basic elements of effective strategizing:

*Capture a Clear Vision of What You Want*

Your vision is a vivid description of where you want to end up. It describes how things look, taste, sound, smell, and feel.

*Describe Your Current Reality*

Here is where you take a critical look at how close you are to your vision. There are two parts to this step:

What do you already have in place? For instance, if you already have all the talent you need, give yourself credit. Walk your way through each of the 8 areas of personal exploration and introspection.

What's missing? If you weren't missing a few things, your vision would already be your reality! Walk your way through each of the 8 areas of personal exploration and introspection of Step #1.

*Based on "What's Missing," Choose Your First Action Step*

Imagine a beautiful garden path that leads you from where you are now (current reality) to where you want to be (your vision). This path is full of stepping-stones that are based on what's missing from your current reality. These stepping-stones are action steps that you know you need to take to complete your journey.

For now, you may only need to describe your first action step (and maybe a few others.) Ultimately, you'll want to fully plan the entire path as clearly as you can.

**Career-Specific Tips for Your Strategizing Process**

I'm feeling compelled to remind you of a few more valuable tips to make sure that your strategizing journey is fun and rewarding. Remember that...

• Career transitions never require irresponsibility.

• There's never one prescribed timeframe for when you should make the leap.

• If you're unsure of an element of your strategy, take a step back and get the information you need to make a good choice.

• There is always a solution for every perceived obstacle.

• Stay true to your gut feelings.

**How long 'til you make the leap?**

Another misconception that we need to address is that you have to be willing to make the leap directly from where you are now into your perfect work.

This is a little like suggesting that a woman cut her waist-length hair directly into a pixie cut. The better advice: Don't do it!

The actual leap to your perfect work likely won't come until you've set the stage with several practice runs.

To make this concept a bit simpler, and significantly aid your strategizing process, take a look at the possibilities inherent in this model:

**The Four Modes of Work**

On the path to perfect work, you can set yourself up for success by remembering that it's a process with no predetermined timetable. Often, people worry that they will not be able to make it financially if they do work they love. But pursuing your ideal work never requires irresponsibility. Depending on the choices you make, you may need to move into one of the following job modes:

**Survival Jobs** – often pay the bills, get you to make a change, or just keep you busy. Usually lasts 3-6 months.

**Interim Jobs** – pay the bills, are a step in the right direction. Usually last 6-18 months. Buys you more time to figure out what you really want to be doing—but at least there's something about it that makes it worthwhile.

**Transitional Jobs** – definite step in the right direction, helps you acquire knowledge and experience for your ideal work. Usually lasts 18-24 months.

**Perfect Work** – you've made it! Lasts indefinitely. But you might want to review things every five years or so. As you grow and evolve, your career hopes will, too.

It's also important to realize that the four modes are not necessarily a linear progression. You can dance around within the four modes of work throughout your lifetime. Any time you re-evaluate your career, you may find yourself opting for one of the modes as part of your strategic plan.

One assumption that many people make is that a survival job means "low paying." Not true. I've met many people who have really great paying survival jobs, and I have experienced it myself. The essential factors of a survival job include buying you some time to align with your next move and keeping you solvent.

It helps to know which mode you're in and which one you're moving to, because it can help you keep perspective throughout the process. It's always easier to hang in there when you can see the method to the madness. Having a clear vision and a sound strategy is what makes a risk a smart one.

Smart risks are good—dumb risks are not. It's a good idea to be able to tell the difference!

\*\*\*\*\*\*\*\*\*\*\*\*\*\*\*\*\*

That's it! You're ready to dive into the strategizing process. Relax, have fun, and remember that you're always in the driver's seat.

## *Anissa's Story*
## Strategically Throwing Out the
## Baby with the Bathwater

What do you do when you're one of those women who can do anything she puts her mind to, so you're extremely successful at your job, but it doesn't make you happy? How do you walk away from all that success and start over in something new?

Meet Anissa. Beautiful, funny, and smart as a whip. When Anissa participated in my weekend career workshop, she was completely burned out by her job but was hesitant to leave the people she loved working with and was worried that a major transition would be too financially challenging.

Anissa says, "I knew that while I had a very promising career path with my company, I was not truly happy."

### Anissa's Journey to a New Career

During the course of the career workshop, Anissa's true calling became quite clear. In the past, she had toyed with the idea of becoming an ultrasound technician. Unfortunately, she felt that too many obstacles stood between her and the fulfillment of this dream.

"I was the mother of two young children and my husband and I were paying off numerous loans. Our financial obligations were really significant. It was hard to seriously consider creating even more debt."

To make matters worse, neither her educational nor her professional background had anything to do with the medical field. And when Anissa had previously researched ultrasound training programs, none were available in her city.

Still, she knew that something had to change, despite all these unfavorable circumstances.

She says, "After a few weeks of true soul searching, I began to look again for some kind of a program that would support my dream career."

### Anissa's Career Epiphany

Anissa made an appointment to speak to the director of the X-ray program at the local community college. Her thought was to explore a program in a related field, hoping she could segue into ultrasound. Imagine her amazement when she walked in to talk to the academic advisor and was told that the college was establishing a brand new program in ultrasound certification.

### Anissa's Transition Plan

"The next day my mind was made up, and I took off work to enroll in Anatomy and Physiology.

I spent that evening figuring out what our real monetary needs were to make ends meet on a monthly basis. I figured that 4 months working to pay off our extra bills and cutting back would get us to the point that we could 'make ends meet' during the time I was in school. This meant that the boys would not be in day care for a year—until I was officially in ultrasound school full-time. My classes would have to be taken at night for the time being. I just knew that I wanted this bad enough that I would make it work someway! I had a plan. The following day, I told my boss that I would stay on for the next 6 months to get us through the busiest time and to train someone. This would allow me to pay off bills and get my mind around school. Then I went home to tell my husband. I had not discussed any of this with him! He took it pretty well and was supportive once he saw that I had a financial plan.

I applied to the program, and was eventually accepted into the first graduating class."

### Where is Anissa now?

I asked Anissa if the plan worked and here's what she said:

"For the most part. I was accepted to ultrasound school for the next year, and of course this meant lots of expenses: daycare, tuition, books, etc.

I had paid off all the short-term debt prior to the beginning of ultrasound school, so I charged tuition and books to the credit cards and began monthly payments. Fortunately, by the time the next semester rolled around I had paid off the prior semester. We cut out home improvements, eating out, skiing, vacations, etc. Surprisingly, the pieces just fell together. That was another way I knew I had done the right thing. I was in school a total of 3 years. I landed a job 3 weeks after graduating— on my second interview. I have never looked back. I love my job and my patients. I cannot describe the feeling that I had the day that I discovered that the ultrasound program had just started and that it was now a possibility. It was in that moment that I knew for sure what my passion was. It was in no way easy....but I would do it a thousand times over.

Here I am, 9 years later, managing a department and loving every minute of my life!"

### Anissa's Advice

"You may have to get pretty creative to make everything work out. Don't worry if it seems impossible; I'm living proof that you can take some pretty tough circumstances and turn them in your favor. You just have to believe in your dream and believe in yourself enough to see the path."

\*\*\*

**Want to hear more of Anissa's Story?  Listen to the audio of Anissa describing her career journey at**

**www.Start2Bloom.com**

\*\*\*

# PART III

# CAREER EVOLUTION:

*Create Your Job Security*

# CHAPTER 12

## *Pruning for New Growth*

**Step #7: Take Charge of Your Career**

"Even if you're on the right track,

you'll get run over if you just sit there."

-- Will Rogers

In October of 2008, tens of thousands of mortgage brokers went to bed feeling as though they had great careers. The next morning they awoke to a debacle. The rug had been ripped out from under them and the biggest question was, "Now what?"

I don't want that to happen to you—ever.

It's true, we live in volatile times. As I've said a number of times, the world of work is changing incredibly quickly and somewhat unpredictably.

So what's the best way for you to create lifelong job security?

Don't pretend that you can put your career—even if you're in your perfect work—on autopilot and that everything will be just fine!

And don't just think about your career when your current job is about to (or already has) ended. Instead, take an active approach to nurturing your career and literally create it for yourself.

**The Care and Feeding of a Career Progression Plan**

Here's some really great news: You are in charge of your own career!

Gone are the days when folks were completely reliant on the whims of the powers that be in some large corporation. Whether it was your immediate boss or someone much higher up, in the past you may have felt as though someone else had all the control.

With the right attitude and some careful planning, you can assure yourself the only true job security that anyone can ever have…

…A compelling vision that creates its own motivation!

**Capture Your Career Vision**

In the last chapter we talked about capturing your vision as part of your strategy for making the leap to your perfect work.

In this section, I'm talking about capturing your vision for your overall career.

In order to do this, you'll need to commit to staying completely aware of the trends in your industry. But guess what? This won't be hard because you've been smart enough to establish a pet project with a virtual home and you are well connected to the movers and shakers in your industry.

By keeping these relationships alive and well, you ensure that you will be hip to whatever is blowing in your industry's wind. And that means you'll be able to forecast the ideal conditions for your career progress.

You'll also need to take into consideration the aspects of yourself that you want to further develop. Do you see yourself becoming more skilled in a particular talent? Do you see yourself applying your talent in more than one industry over time? Do you want to allow different values to come to the forefront and become an orienting factor?

Without question, we each have an imperative to continue to grow and develop ourselves. Without this growth, the meaning and fulfillment slowly begins to erode from even the brightest of careers.

Don't let yourself get caught in a downward spiral. Stay in touch with your own needs, wants, and wishes and tie them into your vision for your career future.

## Do an Annual Review

If you've ever worked in corporate America, undoubtedly you've been subjected to the delights of the annual review or employee performance appraisal.

Supposedly, this evaluation is a component of guiding and managing an individual's career development. If your experience of this phenomenon is anything other than completely positive, you might have a little trouble seeing the merits of conducting this (in a more productive way) for yourself.

Nonetheless, I'm suggesting that you give your career (not your performance) an annual review!

Regularly evaluating how far you've come, on an annual basis, can be a big eye-opener to your next best move in your career progression. Did you come as far as you wanted to this year? What helped or what stood in your way? Can you overcome any current obstacles? Who would be ideal to bring on board as an accomplice? What objectives do you want to set for yourself in terms of your own personal and professional development?

Another thing: although above I've been extolling the merits of an *annual* career progression review, *at any given time* you might begin feeling a bit of a tug to reassess your career situation.

It's important not to ignore these urges.

My client Leissa found herself seriously miserable in her current job. She'd been in the same industry for nearly 30 years, but things had recently changed dramatically because of governmental policy changes.

Leissa found herself waking up every morning with a knot in her stomach and a sense of dread about the coming day. She wondered if it was time to make a major career change.

We sat down and reviewed everything she knew about herself based on the work she did in Step #1 of the Plant Yourself Where You Will Bloom approach.

Leissa realized that she still loved the industry she was in and felt connected to the difference she was making, but that she was no longer using her greatest talents on a daily basis.

She immediately formulated a plan to turn this around, and within a few months she'd made the necessary changes to her work.

And you know what? It worked. One day not long ago, she called and confided in me that she'd recently found herself alone in the elevator on the way to her office and decided to shout, "I love my job!"

We all come equipped with an intuitive capacity that guides us along our life path.

One of the biggest prompts can come when we are about to encounter a changing window of opportunity in our life. Let's look a little closer at what this actually means.

## Consider Your Windows of Opportunity

In our society, we're often accustomed to defining the stages of life according to our age.

We start out as infants, and then we become toddlers. Then we're school age. Then adolescents. Then teenagers. Then young adults. Before we know it, we're in middle age. And then suddenly we're in our golden years.

Our career goes through stages, as well. But rather than age, those stages are usually defined by our life's circumstances. All too often, we choose jobs based on our current situation.

As a kid, we chose from whatever was available to us...baby-sitting, paper route, dog walking.

Once we turned 16, it was mostly retail and restaurants. Sometimes the family business.

After high school, it depended more on education and experience. Because we were young, we started at the bottom and hoped to work our way up.

But now? What window of opportunity are you in now? What kinds of life circumstances are shaping your options and shining a light on the perfect path?

Maybe you're now an empty nester. Maybe you're just beginning to think about having kids. Maybe you're divorcing.

All of these circumstances present you with a set of parameters that may be very different than the lifestyle you've left behind. And sometimes you can foresee that a window may be opening now that will close in a few years, so you need to make the most of it. Or maybe you need to accept that a window is permanently closed (American Idol doesn't take applicants over the age of 28!)

Here's an important truth: no matter what your window looks like... it's always one of opportunity!

**Making choices based on your window of opportunity**

In crafting your career progression plan, there are a couple of notable circumstances that make it helpful to assess your options against your current window of opportunity:

*You have a lot of interests you could explore*

If you're the kind of person who would enjoy learning a little about a lot of different topics, it may be hard to choose! Knowing your current window of opportunity can often naturally narrow the choices.

For example, if you see that the current business climate lends itself well to pursuing a particular interest you have—well, your next move may be pretty obvious. Better to pursue it now, or lose the opportunity forever.

*You can't explain why something doesn't sound as good anymore*

Maybe you had something you were passionate about for a very long time. And now you're just not feeling it anymore. What's going on here? Well, it might be tied in to a recent change in your life.

For example, let's say you were passionately involved in home-schooling your children. You voraciously consumed every bit of information for several years and became an expert. But now your kids have left home, and the fire has basically sputtered out.

Makes sense, when you consider your new window of opportunity!

It's good to know that it's time to move on, and that it's not a lack of commitment on your part.

*You're trying to assess whether to go back to school*

Some people love formal education and some people don't. The decision to go back to school is never one to take lightly.

Once you've found your sweet spot—which means you've identified your perfect work—you may realize that you have an option as to whether to pursue more education or not. Your window of opportunity might be pointing to one decision or the other…things like government loans, levels of competition in programs, or training being offered at your local college at a certain time may each point to the obvious window of opportunity for you.

I could list dozens of examples of windows of opportunity, but the truth is, once you're aware of this dynamic, you'll be able to spot yours pretty easily.

## Possible Elements of Your Career Progression Plan

I don't want to leave this concept without sharing a few things to consider when crafting your plan:

*Graduating to Self-Employment*

You may or may not feel that you have the constitution to attempt self-employment. I'm here to tell you that it's not as scary as you think.

If you want to create the ultimate in job security, learning how to create your own money can't be beat!

Once you understand the bottom-line skill set of self-employment, you can apply it to many, many different professional situations. This means you'll never again be reliant on someone else to create an opportunity for you to make money. You'll be able to create your own revenue-generator with the drop of a new idea!

### *Deliberately Changing Careers*

I once read about a woman who had so many different careers that she wanted to try that she consciously decided to change careers every 5 years.

No matter where she was in her current career, at the five-year mark she put on the brakes and hopped into a completely new vehicle.

This may sound risky, but if you plan to make a new leap (instead of having the need for it sneak up on you and catch you by surprise) you'll be perfectly poised in every way.

### *Embracing the Dead-End*

What do you do when you've taken a job or a career direction as far as it can possibly go? Do you have to panic or fall into a depression? Absolutely not. If you can see the writing on the wall, you can allow yourself to embrace the inevitable demise and ride the wave as far as it will take you.

Perhaps you can even allow yourself to take a voluntary sabbatical and use the opportunity to reinvent yourself. Imagine a bright, shiny new you deciding to take on the world in a whole new way!

### *Self-Initiating Training*

Don't forget that all work and no play makes for a dull career.

If you're highly focused on only getting trained in areas that directly apply to your work, you might be missing a goldmine of possibilities.

For years, I've taught classes in the community education program of our local community college. I'm always amazed, as I peruse each new catalogue, to see the wide range of course offerings.

As you're planning your training for your career progression plan, consider the option to take a completely unrelated course. It might just stimulate your creativity and have you producing some truly original work.

******************

You've come a long way, my African Violet friend!

You've just walked down a beautiful garden path for career success in the wonderful new world of work!

Congratulations!

You're ready for anything now…but do you know what to do first?

Have no fear!

The perfect first action step is just a page turn away. And remember, every truly great journey begins with a single step in the right direction.

## *Leissa's Story*
### Doing What I Do
### The Way I Want to Do It

What do you do when you've worked for decades in a field you love and then the entire industry, including the way you do your job, is forced to change almost overnight?

In fact, everything changes so much, so fast, that it reminds you of when an amateur magician is attempting the Big Finale, where he is supposed to rip a tablecloth off of a beautifully set table while leaving the china and stemware perfectly still. Except what happens is that the magician rips off the tablecloth and sends everything flying to shatter on the ground.

Meet Leissa. Clever, an industry expert, and highly committed to her clients. Leissa was a devoted professional in the mortgage industry for over 30 years before the home loan crisis struck in 2008. When she became my client two years later, she had reached a breaking point. "It just became so difficult to do the work that I do… It was just so hard and so challenging and I had to think, 'Maybe I'm not supposed to do this anymore.'"

But with so much doom and gloom about the state of the economy in general, Leissa worried that starting a career in an unfamiliar field would be too daunting of a task. And she didn't really have a vision for herself doing any other kind of work either.

### Leissa's Career Epiphany

Even though it felt like she was in a bit of a Catch-22, Leissa realized that she couldn't let the circumstances around her dictate whether or not she found a way to be content with her work. She loved her industry, and how it helped people, and didn't want to make a major change. Instead, she thought about how she could create a new job description that would let her do the things she loved and offload some of the other details to a support person.

As she put it, "I didn't have to start over in something brand new. I could just try to do what I do the way I want to do it."

### Where is Leissa Now?

Thriving in a new job in a new company in the mortgage industry, Leissa is happier, and more motivated to keep evolving her perfect career and lifestyle. After her leap of faith, she realized she loved her new work so much that she called to tell me, "I was in the elevator going up to my office and, out loud, I said, 'I love my job!'"

She says her willingness to view her options in a new way led her down a "good road" and she has shown herself that she has the potential to take risks that reap huge rewards.

### Leissa's Advice

The glum national economy could have been an excuse for Leissa to deny herself the life she truly desired. While it seemed that all the changes in her industry were pointing her to give up on the mortgage business altogether, Leissa chose to look within herself and found that all she needed was some clarity about what she really loved about her work, and then the commitment to find a work environment that would support her in using her strengths. She saw that with some creativity, she could once again be just as successful as she'd been in the previous 30 years.

"Obviously there's stuff going on in the world… just grab a piece for yourself. Somebody's getting it…it might as well be you."

**\*\*\***

**Want to hear more of Leissa's Story?  Listen to the audio of Leissa describing her career journey at**

**www.Start2Bloom.com**

**\*\*\***

# EPILOGUE

## 3 Smart Actions to Get You Started

# CHAPTER 13

## Action #1: Get Inspired

"Just don't give up trying to do what you really want to do.
Where there is love and inspiration, I don't think you can go wrong."
-- Ella Fitzgerald

One of the most important things to know along the path to perfect work is that inspiration plays a key role in the success of your quest.

The truth is that without inspiration, nothing is accomplished! Absolutely every action that you take happens because you were inspired in some way. Inspiration is a prompt, a catalyst, a marching order.

### Characteristics of Inspiration

The funny thing about inspiration is that we don't have to actively seek it. It's happening all the time—inspiration can literally be found everywhere.

Sometimes people in the arts will talk about waiting for their inspiration to appear, like a muse. They'll say they can't paint or write or act until they get their inspiration.

My experience has been that inspiration is more like a river that flows all around us. If we want to be inspired, we simply have to become more aware of what's going on in our world. If we want to take a drink from a river we have to dip our hand into it, right? Well, similarly, if we want to be inspired, we have to tune into what's going on and then realize what has particular meaning to us.

When something catches our attention—it's important. We can't try to make something be inspiring; our job is actually just to notice what really *is* inspiring to us. When we react strongly to something, chances are good we're being inspired. In fact, our feelings are the portal to identifying authentic inspiration.

The most powerful emotions attached to inspiration are excitement, compassion, curiosity, anger, sadness, and fear. You can see that some of these emotions are positive and some are negative. Without question, the most powerful motivators are positive emotions. These are the ones that call us to our most noble behavior.

A good example of a positive motivator is the excitement my then-13-year-old son Trevor felt when he began exploring the latest Apple computers. Although the model he wanted cost over $1000, the minute he began dreaming about having a laptop that ran both Windows and Apple operating systems, he began taking every odd job he was offered. Within just a few days, he went from having less than 5% of the money he needed to nearly 25%.

So what's a good example of a negative motivator? Well, you probably know someone who was finally inspired enough to lose weight or quit smoking when his or her doctor laid down the law: do it, or you won't live another five years.

In both of these examples, the individual was inspired enough to take action. The difference is how they felt while taking action and how hard it was to sustain it. Goals are much more easily reached when they're inspired by joy and enthusiasm.

One more thing to keep in mind is that different things inspire each of us. This explains why the same story might inspire one person and not another. It's about values. We are most inspired by things that speak to our personal values. Whether it's beauty, family, adventure, fun, or contribution—when something relates to what we most want to express about ourselves, we are inspired by it.

### *Ways to Engage with Inspiration*

You can use the power of inspiration in a couple of different ways.

First is when you don't have a current goal or direction. This is the time to begin to notice what's going on around you. Anything that grabs your attention is a possible source of inspiration. It could be something that you see on TV or hear on the radio, a conversation that you overhear in a coffee shop, or something that you read in a book or a newspaper or an email.

If you're an Oprah fan, you've no doubt seen stories about how one of her viewers was inspired to take action by something he or she saw on her show. One that stands out for me was a nurse who heard about the suffering of young girls in Africa. This woman was so moved by the need she perceived that, the same day she saw the story, she quit her job and volunteered for an organization that sent her to Africa as part of a doctors abroad program.

The second opportunity to use this power is when you already have a goal, but maybe your commitment and energy are flagging. This is the time to actively seek inspirational resources. If you have a favorite motivational speaker, you can listen to a tape. If you have a friend, a mentor, or a coach who never fails to inspire you—get on the phone or pay them a visit! Maybe you have a favorite author whose books remind you, at your very core, who you truly are and what matters to you.

Stories of other people's courage are some of the most popular sources of inspiration. That's why all of the most successful inspirational speakers and authors use real life stories to appeal to their audiences. The library is full of biographies and autobiographies that describe other people's journeys to success, or you can tune into the cable channel A&E, which has a program called "Biography." Reading or watching about others' struggles and successes can help you tap into your own well of inspiration.

### *Honoring Inspiration*

You might be wondering what happens if we ignore what's inspiring us. For one, we might go into reaction mode. We set goals that are based on other people's opinions—the things they think we "should" be doing. Instead of feeling a real connection to whatever it is that we're pursuing, we feel discomfort. Because we're less resourceful in this state of being, everything takes a lot more effort, and we find that our energy and commitment wane fairly quickly.

When we respect this stage and actively engage in it, we take action on the things that really matter to us. As a result, the path to success is much more clear.

*****************

### *Action #1: Create an Inspiration Journal*

Purchase and begin using an "Inspiration Notebook" or Journal.

You can use it simply to keep track of things that inspire you throughout the week, or use it as a journal to discover inspiration…or both! You will use this notebook throughout your path to perfect work. Have fun with this!

# CHAPTER 14

## *Action #2: Assemble Your Support Team*

"Isolation is the real dreamkiller."

-- Barbara Sher

If you're really paying attention while you're reading this book, you'll realize that in an earlier chapter, I disagreed with this Barbara Sher quote.

But it works to make the point of this chapter, and I'm not too proud to be ambiguous!

What does it all mean?

Simply, if you try to go it alone on this grand adventure, you're likely to get stuck and stay stuck, but good!

Stuck = a dream killed

Support = a dream realized

Which one of those sounds good to you?

### Cheerleaders

To prevent the death of your perfect work dream, why not take a cue from every high school, college, and professional sports program? When the crowd is cheering wildly, the team gets fired up! Who starts all that wild cheering? The cheerleaders, of course!

For our purposes, you are the team that we want to see win. Your cheerleaders are the people surrounding you.

Let's take a look at the traits, qualities, and characteristics of your ideal cheerleaders:

### *They are truly supportive, not just saying they are!*

People don't mean to be deceptive, but the closer they are to you and your situation, the more likely they are to get nervous about the fact that you are planning to change.

Did you know that people hate it when another person changes? It's true. Their first reaction is to try to get you to change back to who you used to be. They do this because they're worried about how your relationship will change and are nervous that you will not share the same level of intimacy.

You probably have a gut feeling about who you know that will be truly supportive, and who is more likely to only pay lip service to it. Trust your gut.

### *They are creative*

Fran Lebowitz said, "Great people talk about ideas, average people talk about things, and small people talk about wine."

I have nothing against wine—I rather enjoy it, actually. But when I am in the midst of making a dream come true, I want to benefit from the great ideas of other people.

When you invite great, creative people to join your dream team, you open the door to letting your grand adventure take spectacular twists and turns. You will likely see yourself accomplishing far more than you ever expected.

And then you can drink some wine to celebrate!

### *They are ambitious*

If you are a woman, you will definitely appreciate what my friend Glenda once told me, "The word is ambitious, not am-bitch-es!"

Don't be afraid to bring on cheerleaders who are ready to go after big things in life.

Even if they seem like they are aiming for bigger things than what you're after, you will feel yourself being naturally pulled forward by their energy.

You don't have to worry about things going too far; you will always be in the driver's seat and that means you're in control of both the accelerator and the brake.

### *They are optimistic*

Craig Valentine, motivational speaker extraordinaire, mentions that one of the reasons he won Salesperson of the Year for 3 out of 4 years was because he stayed away from negative people. Before becoming a full-time professional speaker and executive speech coach, Craig delivered sales presentations for Glencoe/McGraw-Hill and three times won the Mid-Atlantic Division's Salesperson of the Year award. He sold more than $8 million in educational resources in one year and reached sales of up to 233% of goal.

Take his experience to heart. Optimistic people are natural problem-solvers. They don't see obstacles as anything but circumstances to overcome.

Neither should you!

*They believe in you*

Someone believing in you is different than someone loving you, caring about you, or simply wanting the best for you.

When someone believes in you, they know—without question—that you can do it. The shadow of doubt never crosses their mind.

This is the kind of energy that eradicates your own doubts about your abilities. As a result, you will keep moving forward.

Worth its weight in gold, I tell ya.


**Ideal Candidates**


Just exactly who would be the ideal mix of people on your support team? Let's take a look at some possibilities:


*A Mentor*

If you've never had a mentor, you are in for a real treat!

A mentor is someone who is at least a few steps (but ideally many, many steps) further down the same path you are following. They have literally "been there, done that" and can give you insight as to the lay of the land.

Their experience will cut your learning curve multifold.


*A Coach*

All great athletes have a coach. They wouldn't dream of stepping onto the playing field without this particular kind of guidance and experience.

Why would you?

A great coach will know how to help you develop yourself to reach your full potential. He or she will ask you the tough questions, challenge you to do and be more, and help you hold the vision of where you're heading.

Look for your own professional career coach, someone who is trained and certified, to help you identify your strengths, areas for growth, and who can provide you with the structure, strategy, and support you need to win your career game.

### *A Buddy*

If you want to make sure you never feel alone on the journey, nothing beats having a fellow traveler.

A buddy is someone who is also seeking to discover her own perfect work.

She can share with you all the triumphs and tribulations along the way. Just when you are discouraged, she will have a big win and keep you inspired to keep moving forward. And of course, it will work the other way, too.

### *A Counselor*

A good friend of mine once said, "There are only two kinds of people in the world. Those who are in counseling, and those who should be!"

Let go of the misconception that you have to be damaged goods to benefit from the help of a good counselor.

Very often it's irrational fears and doubts that can stand in the way of making progress on achieving your hopes and dreams.

A great counselor can help you create new emotional pathways that change limiting habits and patterns of thinking.

### *A Spiritual Advisor*

No matter your spiritual beliefs, when you're taking on this big of a challenge, it helps to be reminded of the bigger picture.

### *Other possible support team members*

Since this kind of work requires a great deal of energy, you might consider including a nutritionist, a personal trainer, a naturopath, and anyone else who helps you stay physically fit and mentally strong.

*****************

### *Action #2: Make a List of Your Support Team*

Now it's your turn…who else do you think would help you stay the course?

Don't hesitate to build the strongest team of supporters that you can possibly imagine.

After all, everybody loves to be on the winning team!

# CHAPTER 15

## *Action #3: Take Step #1*

"If I am not for myself, who will be for me?

If I am not for others, what am I?

If not now, when?"

--Rabbi Hillel

If not now, when?

Indeed, Rabbi Hillel, indeed.

*****************

*Action #3: Go Back to Chapter 6*

Dear African Violet,

It's Time to Plant Yourself Where You Will Bloom!

You can do it.

I believe in you.

(And as my brilliant mother would say, "God Bless.")

# *FREE*
# "FULL BLOOM STARTER KIT"

Jennifer Anderson and the Full Bloom Career Academy
Invite You and a Friend
To register for the free Full Bloom Starter Kit
For more information and to register, please visit
**www.Start2Bloom.com**

Here's what you'll receive:
- **Free E-copy of the acclaimed book:**
  *Plant Yourself Where You Will Bloom*
  How to turn what makes you unique into a meaningful and lucrative career
- **Free Career Training:**
  "Who Do You Think You Are?" An introductory guide to discovering what makes you unique and how to turn it into a lucrative and rewarding career
- **Free Career Audio Training:**
  "The 3 Biggest Mistakes Smart Women Make and what You Can Do Instead"
- **$100 Scholarship:**
  Applicable to any career training offered by Full Bloom Career Academy
- **Free Client Success Story Recordings:**
  Listen as Jennifer's most successful clients personally describe their journeys to meaningful and lucrative careers

**www.Start2Bloom.com**

# ACKNOWLEDGEMENTS

I used to look at the acknowledgements sections of books and wonder why it took so darn many people to make such a compact thing happen. Now I have a very different perspective.

I want to thank, first and foremost, my children Laura and Trevor Anderson. You've always believed that what I was doing was important and gave me the space and time to figure it all out! I wouldn't be where and who I am without your unconditional love, encouragement, friendship and support.

Thank you to…

My father, Harry Gibbons. I know you don't want to be acknowledged, but it wouldn't feel right to leave you out. You're the best coach I've ever had.

My brother, Greg Gibbons, for the Friday morning doses of laughter, perspective, and dreaming. And his wife, Shirley, for always saying she "doesn't know how I do it" and for inspiring me with her incredible design talent.

My sister, Theresa Gibbons, who has always been a rock for me. My sisters, Mary Lee, Betsy, Susan and Kathy, who've loved me even when I wasn't even slightly lovable and support me exactly how I need it whenever I need it.

My best friend, Anissa Speight, who really showed me the power of a career epiphany and never ever, even once, doubted anything I've ever said or done—no matter how squishy the idea.

Pete Anderson and my grandson Holden Anderson, who've made very special contributions in my world.

John Goalby, my friend, accountability partner, and all-around remarkable human being.

Ruth Harshfield, who has stood by me when the worst of storms blew through and who throws the best wild game feed on the planet.

John Sheldon, my first client, and Stephanie Arnheim, who have believed in me from minute one.

DeeDee Remington, my second client and the definition of creativity.

My fellow TimberTalker Toastmasters, Leissa, Tom, Rick, Deanna, Cathy, Jane, Cathey and so many more who have witnessed the evolution of Coach Jen and become my friends, clients, and champions. The word of the day is "sesquipedalian."

My coaching colleagues and friends, Prataap Patrose, Sarah Uchytil, Michelle Kelso, Kent Blumberg, Carla Hugo, Chi Wai Ning, Lynn Hess (who is also my editor), Diane Bonneau, Andrea Novakowski, Chrissy Carew, Cinder Ernst, and Michelle Payne. You've modeled the highest standards of professionalism, compassion, and creativity.

My extraordinary intern Natalie Humphrey who played a key role in writing my client's success stories.

My clients over the years, who have inspired me and taught me more than I ever expected. I've always said that I attract the coolest people on the planet, and every single one of you has proven me right.

And finally, you, my future African Violet. I may not have met you yet, but you've been inspiring me from afar…

# African Violet Wisdom

Some of my favorite African Violets offered to contribute words of wisdom to inspire and sustain you on your journey to meaningful and lucrative work. Here is what they wanted to share with you…

### From Marnie Bench

www.marniebenchcoaching.net

"My favorite encouraging reminder is this- wishing is not the same as doing- so do it! I realized one day that my journals seemed to be filled with sentences that started with the words 'I wish...' and in reality I could have changed them all to 'I can...'

Have a beautiful day! You have my support…"

********

### From Donna Internicola

www.envisionpossibility.com

"Be not the slave of your own past. Plunge into the sublime seas, dive deep and swim far, so you shall come back with self-respect, with new power, with an advanced experience that shall explain and overlook the old."

~ Ralph Waldo Emerson

### From Sarah Uchytil

www.sarahucoach.com

"Gratitude, Joy and Appreciation are the 3 greatest gifts you can give yourself. With a daily practice of what you are grateful for, who brought joy to your life, and what you appreciate about yourself, more wonderful gifts will continue to flow into your life."

********

### From Nani Stuckman

"In my experience, attitude means a lot! A lot of times when you are ready for a career shift, it comes from being in a bad situation which leads to feelings of frustration and you may not have the best attitude. In essence, you may not display the person you want to be or the person you want to portray to the potential new company or new opportunity.

However, when you take the first step (even if it's tiny) and you are out there exploring opportunities, you are changing your thinking from the negative current state to the possibilities and to the positive. This shift not only helps you with the next step in your career search, but it also makes your current situation a more positive one. I believe that it will make you a better candidate, interview better, and just be a happier person in the process of getting to your next step."

********

### From Michelle Kelso

www.etjcoaching.com

"Nobody can go back and start a new beginning, but anyone can start today and make a new ending."

~ Maria Robinson

### From Kent Blumberg

www.kentblumberg.com

"Trust your passion!"

********

### From Kelly Ikenberry

www.kellyikenberry.com

"Never forget that at the center of fulfillment is 'Fill Me'. Dare to discover your fulfillment factors, take actions to include them in work and life, and enjoy what you've designed!"

********

### From Jean Hausmann

www.jeanhausmann.com

"Success requires that our aim become a burning desire, followed with a strategy and plans of how to deal when motivation wanes."

********

### From Gunilla Janmark Veldhuis

www.gunillajanmarkcoaching.se

"They both had their own inner beauty. One of them came from a lukewarm environment where feelings were absent - she was like a pearl, the other was the result of condensed pressure mixed with hot emotions - she was like a diamond. Both journeys had been accompanied by both pain and struggle but looking at them, you could see their inner shine - their work was carrying beautiful fruits that they joyfully shared with the world. And so will you once you decide and stay with it."

*******

### From Elvira Hopper

www.elvirahopper.com

"When you discover what it is that you TRULY LOVE and were BORN TO DO...you will LEAP FROG over the competition... who may have more experience or education than you."

Shakespeare said,

"Parting is such sweet sorrow..."

But we don't have to part!


Stay Connected to Jen and Plant Yourself Where You Will Bloom:


**www.Start2Bloom.com**

9978851R00102

Made in the USA
San Bernardino, CA
01 April 2014